My Guardian Angel, My Best Friend

My Guardian Angel, My Best Friend

Stories for children

Lorna Byrne

Illustrated by Aideen Byrne

CORONET

First published in Great Britain in 2020 by Coronet
An Imprint of Hodder & Stoughton
An Hachette UK company

2

A CIP catalogue record for this title is available from the British Library

Hardback ISBN 9781473635968
eBook ISBN 9781473635951

Typeset in Sabon MT by Hewer Text UK Ltd, Edinburgh
Printed and bound in Great Britain by Clays Ltd, Elcograf, S.p.A.

Hodder & Stoughton policy is to use papers that are natural, renewable
and recyclable products and made from wood grown in sustainable
forests. The logging and manufacturing processes are expected to
conform to the environmental regulations of the country of origin.

Hodder & Stoughton Ltd
Carmelite House
50 Victoria Embankment
London EC4Y 0DZ

www.hodder.co.uk

This book is for all the children in the world
who hear the whispers of their guardian angel.

CONTENTS

Previous Publications

Angels in My Hair

Stairways to Heaven

A Message of Hope from the Angels

Love from Heaven

*The Year with Angels: A Guide to
Living Lovingly through the Seasons*

*Prayers from the Heart: Prayers for Help and
Blessings, Prayers of Thankfulness and Love*

*Angels at My Fingertips:
The Sequel to Angels in My Hair*

INTRODUCTION

By Aideen Byrne

Dear readers (and parents of readers),

Many of you will have come to this book having already read some or all of Lorna Byrne's previous publications. You will have encountered me within those pages under a pseudonym: Megan, Lorna's youngest child. Lorna asked me to write this introduction to her children's book and to illustrate it. I'll refer to Mam as Lorna throughout this introduction. I want to speak about Lorna in a way that reflects all of who she is, to me and to all of you. She told me that the angels, including my guardian angel, said that I would be the best person to do this because I grew up with a belief in my guardian angel. In a world that often mocks these things, Lorna gave me permission to believe.

This is essentially the purpose of this book as well – to remind children that they have a guardian angel and to help them to stay connected to the spiritual side of themselves. Lorna has always been a wonderful spiritual resource and guide (as well as being my mam and all that encompasses) to me, and also to many people all around the world. I am grateful to share some of the wisdom I received from her as a child. I am particularly attached to the story of Suzy, which I heard many times growing up. Mam told me the story often as I asked her to repeatedly. I refer to Suzy as the Daisy Chain Girl.

These stories are for children who are spiritual, but also for those who are not. That is paramount. This book is to encourage children to experience the spiritual side of life. Any beliefs are secondary to that. So, whether you are reading this as someone who believes in angels or someone who likes to read about a magical world where children are not alone and have help every day, in every moment – welcome!

For both of us, it was important that through writing and illustrating these stories we connected to our childhood selves and created a book that spoke from that part of us. While these stories are fictional, they are inspired by real-life events. We hope that you see your childhood selves in them too. We didn't want to create a book about children going on grand adventures (even though those are of course fun) but rather, something that is more reflective of real life. Each story is about children doing normal things with their guardian angel alongside them.

Both the title and the illustration on the cover draw from two real-life children. The title was inspired by a young boy who was a very special friend to Lorna and our whole family. Lorna first met this young boy at one of her events. He had read *Angels in My Hair* and had travelled with his parents from the hospital to Lorna's event because he wanted to see her in person. Lorna noticed him immediately as he was clearly ill and had many medical supports in place. The angels told her not to draw attention to him, but Lorna couldn't understand why the audience wasn't paying more attention to this young boy. When it came to the question and answers portion of her talk, the boy stood up and said, 'My guardian angel is my best friend.' He had no qualms or hesitation when it came to admitting or declaring this – unlike many others in the audience. I know that in the future Lorna wants to share with you more about this special young boy, if she can. For now, we titled this book in his memory. I am glad he came into our lives, even for a short while, and I find solace that he is with God and all the angels and that he is at peace. As someone who has lost loved ones and believes they are at peace with God, and that sometimes they are around us, supporting us, I always feel that it is those left behind who I need the most sympathy. To Noah's family and friends, I say we love you.

The cover illustration draws on my childhood. If you have read any of Lorna's books, you will know my father died when I was four years old. When Lorna was out working and my brothers and sister weren't at home, Daddy (I never called him anything else and changing now would seem wrong) would look after me. After Daddy passed away, our neighbour spoke to Lorna about how she saw my father in the back garden pushing me on the swing at a time when he was terminally ill and had only a few days to live. This was a tremendous feat for someone so near death's door. Lorna has told me that she knows the angels were helping him, including his guardian angel, so that he could get out of bed and push me on the swing. It felt right to me to pay homage to Daddy in this book, probably because I have thought so much about my childhood and spent many evenings speaking with Lorna about it. I was inspired to draw on this moment from my life because I think adults often see children as being without fear; that they have a sense of being indestructible. I remember from my own childhood that this is not always the case. Our hope is that these stories will help you, the children, to be brave.

Aideen – age 5 or so, on swing in back garden.

I know many parents or loved ones of children have wanted Lorna to publish a children's book for a long time. I've met many of those people. Speaking to them now, and to other adults in general, I want to say that this book is intended above all to remind any child who reads it that they have a guardian angel. Lorna has talked frequently about how all younger children can see angels, especially their guardian angel. I sometimes wonder how many 'imaginary friends' are really guardian angels. The way we live today chases that spirituality from children. But parents should not be afraid to let their children believe in their guardian angel as that belief should be there throughout their life, helping them – as it has been for me. As a child, I never questioned having a guardian angel. I remember playing with her. Perhaps this book can help children to remember and know the presence of their guardian angel. Maybe it will have a similar impact on adults as well. Spirituality brings a strength that life often requires us to draw on. Living – thriving – is easier when you're not alone, when you are loved and supported.

Another thing I would like to draw your attention to is Lorna's dyslexia. I am always in awe of how she has written so many beautiful books that are international bestsellers, despite her dyslexia and lack of schooling. In 1950s Ireland, dyslexia was not recognised, so instead, Lorna was considered 'retarded' and denied education from about the age of ten. If you take nothing else from this book, take the fact that it was written by a woman with a learning difficulty, someone who only had a few years of schooling. We know that there are often many barriers, both within and outside our control, to achieving our dreams, and living a life that is meaningful, brings us joy and is full of love. I hope this book helps you to see the light of hope that is in front of you.

I was very afraid of making myself vulnerable through writing this introduction and illustrating these stories. In the midst of writing this, I panicked. This was partly because I was juggling this as a side project to my full-time work, while in the middle of a pandemic, but also because of all the uncertainty that making a part of oneself public brings. But it was also due to the anxiety that making a part of oneself public brings. Lorna helped me to remember that there is purpose in putting my heart into this art – for the children. I remember being bullied. I remember being afraid to go on stage to dance. I know what it is like to be ill and isolated (an experience very different to Suzy's and I try to count my blessings every day). I remember worrying about my mam, and the list of what I recognise and relate to within the pages of this children's book goes on.

I never liked children's stories. From a very young age I read adult books. Partly because of my reading ability, but also because I never saw myself reflected in children's stories. I hope this book adds itself to what I hope will be a growing body of children's stories that encourage, build up and draw on children's real lives.

I wanted to depict the guardian angel of each child within this book with authenticity. I think mistakenly we often lend ourselves to seeing angels as those more traditional, holy depictions. I'm sure you know the type. But Lorna describes angels as taking on a human-like form for our comfort. I think when a child sees their guardian angel, it often appears like a human being but maybe with colourful clothes, interesting hair ... perhaps wings for fun. Lorna has told me that the appearance of our guardian angels often reflects something we need. If we need to be strong (mentally or physically), our guardian angel might look like a warrior. If we need to connect more to our feminine or masculine side, our angel might reflect what we need most. Perhaps our guardian angel sometimes takes on a form that reminds us of what we need to accept – or to work on. I know Lorna says mine has a tendency to mimic pulling her hair out ... and I know that is because I need to work on being present and not letting anxiety and panic take over on the more personally challenging days.

I hope that I was spiritually inspired, and that my heart is reflected in these images. I tried my best to visualise the guardian angel of each child in a truthful, real-to-life way and transcribe that essence into the illustrations. My art has always been something precious and for myself. I feel as if I am letting a fledging out for its first flight. I hope in its passing, it brings you joy.

Love,
Aideen

Jacob and Rebecca

Chapter 1

Grasshopper

Jacob was out in the orchard, talking to his guardian angel. As he shuffled the grass with his feet, all the grasshoppers hopped into the air, some landing on his hand and on his trousers. Jacob burst out laughing, while mimicking the grasshoppers and jumping through the grass and calling out to his guardian angel, 'I love your name because I love grasshoppers as well.'

Jacob's guardian angel whispered in his ear, 'I love it when you call me Grasshopper, Jacob.'

At that moment the sun shone more brightly through the trees and onto the grass. Jacob stopped and looked at a grasshopper on his hand. Because the sun was shining in his eyes, Jacob had to squint but as he did so, he caught a glimpse of his guardian angel dressed in emerald green colours, giving a male appearance. Jacob turned the other way so he could open his eyes more fully, thinking he could then see his guardian angel more clearly, but just then, a cloud drifted in front of the sun. He was disappointed. He could no longer see anything of his guardian angel.

'I never thought of you as a boy with long yellow hair,' Jacob said to Grasshopper, as he stood in the orchard in the long grass. He put his hand to his mouth and gave a little giggle of excitement.

Jacob's guardian angel said to him, 'Angels are neither boys nor girls, but I knew you would love me to look like a boy.'

Jacob said, 'Yes, thank you for allowing me to see you, Grasshopper.'

'You're welcome,' said Jacob's guardian angel. 'Your mother is calling you and your little sister is awake.'

'Oh shucks,' Jacob said in disappointment. 'I thought I would have a little bit more time on my own.'

'You are never on your own Jacob. I'm always with you.'

'I know, Grasshopper,' said Jacob, 'and at least you don't keep on pestering me like my little sister does.'

'Be nice to your little sister Rebecca,' Jacob's guardian angel whispered in his ear.

'I'm always nice to her. I love her so much, but she is just such a pest. She wants everything that belongs to me,' Jacob replied.

Jacob's guardian angel whispered in his ear again, 'Your mum is calling.'

Jacob ran through the long grass, out
of the orchard and through the gate.
'Stop and lock the gate,' his guardian
angel said. 'You must keep your little
sister safe.'

'Thank you,' Jacob replied in a little whisper,
before locking the gate and running into the house.

Jacob was only just through the door when his little
sister screamed at him, 'Where have you been? I have
really missed you, Jacob,' and she gave him a big hug,
saying again, 'I really missed you!'

Jacob thought to himself he better not tell his little
sister Rebecca, that he had been out in the orchard,
talking with his guardian angel Grasshopper. Instead,
he took a little piece of Lego out of his pocket and said
he had been playing with it on the fence. Rebecca
reached up to grab it out of his hand. He held it up as
high as he could and said, 'No, it's mine. You go and
play with your Lego.' But she gave Jacob that look with
her big smile and those pretty eyes and said to her big
brother, 'Please, please!' He gave in and gave the Lego
toy to her. He loved to see her happy and laughing.

Another day, Jacob took some coloured pencils and
paper and sat down at the kitchen table. He started to
draw a picture – something he loved to do. But as soon

as Rebecca saw him doing that, she came over to the table and straight away climbed up onto the chair. She insisted on having Jacob's pencils and the piece of paper he was drawing on. Their mummy came over and said, 'Rebecca, use your own pencil and paper.'

But she insisted, starting to scream, 'No, I want Jacob's. His is better than mine.'

Their mummy said to Jacob, 'Just for a little bit of peace, would you give your drawing and pencils to Rebecca and you can have hers?'

He looked at her with a sad face and said, 'Mum, it's not fair.'

At the same time, his guardian angel whispered in his ear and said, 'Do what your mum said.'

So, Jacob gave Rebecca the picture he was drawing and his pencils. He took the blank page his mum had given

Rebecca drawing on Miley's picture, with Jacob and his guardian angel beside her.

Rebecca, and her pencils. Then he watched as she scribbled all over his drawing.

His guardian angel whispered in his ear, 'She loves you, Jacob. You are her big brother and she wants to do everything you do. She wants to be just like you.'

He spoke to his guardian angel in his mind as he started to draw another picture: 'I wish Rebecca didn't want everything of mine and to be like me.'

A few minutes later, his little sister insisted on having his new picture too. She wanted to draw on the same piece of paper Jacob was drawing on. Jacob jumped down off the chair, waving the picture he had just drawn in the air, shouting at his little sister, 'If you want my picture, you have to catch me!'

Rebecca jumped down off her chair and ran after Jacob laughing and saying, 'I *will* catch you!'

Jacob ran into the front room and hid under a blanket on the couch. The drawing was sticking out from under the blanket. Rebecca jumped on top of him, grabbing the drawing and running out the door and up the stairs. Jacob jumped up and ran after her. The two of them were both screaming and laughing – having great fun.

Later that night, when Jacob was in bed and saying his prayers with his mummy, he asked her if he could have a few minutes to draw a picture before going to sleep. 'Yes, ten minutes,' she said, and then left the room.

Without getting out of bed, Jacob reached under it and pulled out a box. He lifted the lid and took out some colouring pencils and paper. He drew a picture of his little sister and himself splashing in puddles of water with their wellies on. He had almost finished when his guardian angel whispered in his ear, 'You better put your drawing away now. It's time to go to sleep.'

Without hesitation, Jacob did what his guardian angel said and put his drawing back in his box. He slid the box as far as possible under his bed. This is where he kept all his special things that he did not want his little sister to get her hands on.

Just before he went to sleep, he thanked his guardian angel, and just as his eyes were closing, he said, 'I have the best sister in the world.'

Chapter 2

A Garden Tea Party

One sunny day, Jacob said to his mummy, 'You said we could have a garden tea party on the next warm and sunny day.'

She looked at him and said, 'The garden's not big enough.'

Jacob said, 'Mummy, but we could have a garden tea party out on the green.'

Of course, as soon as little Rebecca heard her brother talking about a party, she started to shout, 'Please, Mummy! Please, Mummy!' Their mum gave in and said, 'Okay, this afternoon, but first of all, you have to help me tidy up the house.'

They both looked at their mummy and said, 'Do we have to?'

'Yes, if you want a garden tea party out on the green,' she replied.

'Okay. Where will we start?' asked Jacob, and his mum said, 'In the front room where all your toys are. Sort them all out and tidy them up.'

'Okay,' they said, and off they ran.

It was going on twelve o'clock. The sun was shining really brightly in the sky. It was nice and warm. Jacob said to his mummy, 'Do you think it's getting near time for us to have our tea party out on the green?'

'Yes,' she said. 'Let's gather up all the things. We need a big blanket, fruit and some nice goodies. You get them out of the cupboard.'

Rebecca ran to help as well. 'We'll have them ready!' shouted Jacob.

Their mummy was making some sandwiches when Rebecca said to her mummy, 'Can I ask my friend next door, Mary, to come to the tea party?'

'Could Peter come too?' said Jacob.

Their mummy nodded and said, 'Yes.'

So, Jacob took Rebecca's hand and they went next door. They knocked on the front door and asked if Mary could come to the tea party. 'Yes,' her mummy said.

'We will be going out onto the green in a few minutes,' said Jacob.

Mary was all excited too.

Jacob walked down the road a little further and knocked on another door and asked his friend, Peter, to join them as well. Peter was also delighted to be invited.

A few minutes later, Jacob, Rebecca and their mummy, as well as Mary and Peter, walked over to the green with the blanket. It was full of goodies. As their mummy spread out the blanket on the grass, Jacob and Rebecca sat down. Other parents appeared on the green with their blankets of goodies. It ended up being a big garden party on the local green of their housing estate.

Soon all the children were playing games. There were a few tears at times when someone fell, but it always only ended up being a tiny little scratch They even got their mums and dads to join in, racing and jumping with skipping ropes. Others had hula hoops. Sometimes the children laughed as they watched their parents trying to play the games. Some of the parents looked especially funny when they tried to use the hula hoops. Other parents even said they could jump much higher than the children, but that never happened. The children were better at playing all of the games, even tag chasing, running away from the mothers and fathers, who could never seem to catch them. There was lots of laughter.

All the parents wore themselves out, some saying they had to take a break. Some sat down on the blankets and chatted.

At the end everybody had shared their food with everyone else and there wasn't a sandwich or a piece of fruit or any goody left over. Everything had been eaten.

Once the party had finished, everybody started to clean up. The parents folded up the blankets and the children put all the cups and sweet papers into the baskets. They left the green spotless. There weren't even any crumbs left for the birds.

'We will all have to do this again the next time it's nice and warm,' Jacob and Rebecca's mummy said to some of the other parents as they were packing up.

All the parents agreed and so did the children, jumping for joy.

As Jacob and Rebecca walked back to their house with their mummy, Rebecca was already asking, 'Can we do it again tomorrow?'

'Not for a couple of weeks,' said her mummy. 'I'll talk to some of the parents and see when it will suit them.'

Jacob asked, 'Can I take my bike out and go for a cycle around the estate?'

His mummy said, 'In a few minutes. You have to first clean out the basket and Rebecca has to help you.'

Jacob and Rebecca looked up at their mummy and gave a sigh.

Their mummy said, 'Well, if you ever want to have another garden tea party out on the green with all the other families, you have to do your share as well – which you have done so far, but it's not finished yet. I need the basket cleaned out.'

'Okay,' Jacob and Rebecca said at the same time, with big smiles on their faces. They took the basket from their mummy, put it on the kitchen table and took all the sweet papers out, putting them in the bin. Then they took out the reusable cups to clean. There was a little diluted orange juice left in the bottle, so Jacob asked his mummy if they could share it. 'Yes,' she said.

A few minutes later, they put the basket away and said to their mummy, 'All done.'

Their mummy said, 'You can go out to play now.'

The two of them ran out to play a few minutes later.

After a while Jacob and Rebecca came back into the house and into the kitchen to where their mummy was starting to prepare dinner. 'It's raining,' said Jacob.

Their mummy said, 'Don't be complaining about the rain. We need it. It hasn't rained for a few days.'

Jacob said, 'I wish it wouldn't rain.'

Jacob's mummy turned to him and explained, 'If it didn't rain, there would be no food. The crops wouldn't grow. The animals would have no grass to eat. There would be no fruit on the trees. Everything would wither and die. We need rain and you, Jacob, need water to drink. Water is in all the drinks that we have and if it didn't rain, what would the fish do?'

Jacob said, 'Oh yes, I forgot. But sometimes, Mummy, it seems to rain an awful lot.'

'I know,' said his mummy, 'but it didn't rain when we were having our garden tea party out on the green.'

Jacob smiled and said, 'Yes,' and he went back into the front room, walked over to the window and gazed out, watching the rain falling from the clouds. The sky had darkened just before it started to rain, and now it didn't look as if the rain was going to stop any time soon. Jacob said to his guardian angel, in his mind, 'How right my mummy is all the time.'

Grasshopper whispered in his ear, 'You should always listen to your mummy and dad and do what they tell you. Your mummy is right about the rain. Everything needs water.'

Jacob spoke back silently to his guardian angel, 'Thank you, Grasshopper.' Just then his little sister ran over to him and asked what he was looking at. Jacob said, 'I'm just looking at the rain.'

'It's making everything wet!' said Rebecca, and she started to laugh before saying, 'I would love to go out and play in the rain.'

Jacob looked at her and said, 'Well, Mummy wouldn't allow you because you could get a cold and all your clothes would get wet.'

'It would be like getting into a bath with all my clothes on, Jacob.' She burst out laughing again as they gazed out the window.

Then they saw their dad pull up in the car outside the door. They shouted to their mummy, 'Dad's home!'

Jacob ran to the front door and opened it. Their dad was standing there dripping wet. He said to Jacob and Rebecca, 'I'm soaking coming that little distance from the car to the door. Thank you for having the door open. I would have gotten wetter if I had to put the key in the door and turn the lock.'

Rebecca put her hand out the door and felt some of the drops of rain on her hand and she giggled.

'Close the door now,' said her dad.

Rebecca closed the door and helped her dad lock it. He gave the two of them a big hug.

Mummy said, 'You're home early.'

'The boss said I could go home early as I have to start work at six in the morning.'

Their mummy said, 'Well, dinner won't be ready for a while yet.'

'Great,' said Rebecca. 'So we can play then.'

Mummy said, 'Don't wear your dad out. Remember, he has to be in work at six in the morning.'

'Okay, just a few little games,' said Rebecca.

'All right,' said their dad and the three of them went into the front room to play some games on the floor.

Sometime later, their mummy called for the three of them to set the table. The children moaned as they wanted to continue playing, but their dad said, 'We better obey the boss.'

Jacob got up and ran into the kitchen, followed by his little sister and their dad. They started to set the table and two minutes later, they were all sitting down and having dinner.

When it was bedtime, Rebecca's dad took her up to bed and an hour later, he tucked Jacob into bed as well. His dad said he would be going to bed shortly too.

Jacob said to his dad, 'You and Mummy work very hard.'

His dad said, 'Yes, your mummy and I have to work hard in order to pay the bills, and buy you and Rebecca your presents when your birthdays come around and all the things for school.'

'Thanks,' said Jacob, as he put his arms around his dad.

His dad said, 'Now, let's say a prayer before you go to sleep.'

They did so together and when his dad left the bedroom, Jacob asked Grasshopper to say a prayer with him too. His guardian angel whispered in his ear, 'I always pray with you, Jacob.'

Jacob's prayer was for his mummy and dad and his little sister. Jacob's eyes grew heavy and he fell asleep shortly afterwards. He thought he might hear his dad going up to bed, but he didn't, for Jacob was already asleep.

CHAPTER 3

A SHOPPING TRIP

A few days later, when Jacob was pushing his little sister on the swing, his mummy called out, 'I need you to come in here to get ready. We need to go to the shopping centre.'

The two of them ran into the house. Their mummy said, 'Both of you, wash your face and hands. Jacob, help your sister.'

'No, I can wash my own,' said Rebecca. She made a great attempt at it but didn't quite wash her hands enough. When her mummy went to help her, she pushed her mummy's hands away and said again, 'No, I can do it on my own.'

When she had finished, Rebecca's mummy said, 'Here is the towel. Dry your face and hands, Rebecca.'

A few minutes later, they were all in the car driving to the shopping centre. Jacob asked his mummy, 'Why are we going to the shopping centre?'

At the same time Rebecca said, 'Why Mummy?'

'All of Jacob's trousers are gone too small for him.'

Jacob said, 'Yes, I'm getting new trousers!'

Rebecca said, 'What about me?'

'Lots of your clothes are too small for you as well, Rebecca. Your leggings aren't fitting you anymore and you need some new socks,' said her mummy. Rebecca clapped her hands with delight.

In no time at all, they were at the shopping centre. When they got out of the car, Rebecca's mummy noticed that Rebecca had her special toy with her, a bunny rabbit called Snuggles. It comforted her. Rebecca was always insisting on taking Snuggles with her, but her mummy was afraid it might get lost – and what would they do then? Jacob even helped his mummy to try to convince his little sister to leave Snuggles in the car sitting in her seat, but as usual it didn't work, and so Snuggles was brought along.

Rebecca held Snuggles close to her chest as she walked into the shopping centre with her mummy and brother. Sometimes, Snuggles was stuck into Rebecca's pocket. No one else could carry Snuggles. It wasn't allowed.

Snuggles fell out of Rebecca's pocket and Jacob's guardian angel, Grasshopper, whispered in his ear, 'Snuggles is on the floor, Jacob.'

 Jacob picked Snuggles up and said to his little sister, 'You nearly lost Snuggles.'

She grabbed Snuggles from Jacob and

gave a little whimper, holding him tight to her chest. Jacob stood in front of his little sister and said, 'Don't forget you are carrying Snuggles, Rebecca, because if you do, you will drop him on the floor again and I might not see it, and then Snuggles will be lost. Would you like me to carry him for you instead?'

Rebecca said, 'No,' and she ran after her mummy, who was picking out some socks and leggings for her.

Jacob said to Grasshopper, silently in his mind, 'We're in trouble. She's going to lose Snuggles. I know she is. She will forget she's holding him. Does my little sister ever listen to her guardian angel?'

Grasshopper whispered in Jacob's ear, 'You know your little sister is not very good at listening to you, or your mummy, or your dad, or anybody – never mind her guardian angel. Her guardian angel has a really hard job just keeping her safe, but you help an awful lot because you listen to me.' Jacob smiled when he heard Grasshopper say that.

Jacob's mummy called to him to try on some trousers. He walked over to her and she held the trousers up against him to see if they would fit. His little sister was running around the rails of clothes. Rebecca's mummy said to her, 'Stop running around the shop. You're only meant to walk. The shop assistant will give out to you.'

Rebecca did as her mummy said this time, but she still kept disappearing in among the rails of clothes. Jacob said to himself, 'My little sister definitely doesn't listen to anybody.' Now his mummy grabbed his sister's hand and said, 'Come with us. We're going to the dressing room. Jacob needs to try these trousers on.'

In the dressing room, Rebecca insisted on trying on her leggings as well. Jacob smiled at his little sister as she admired herself in the mirror. He said to her, 'They look pretty on you.'

She smiled shyly back at her big brother and said, 'Thank you. Your trousers look pretty on you too, Jacob.'

Jacob made an expression of horror on his face. 'I'm a boy, Rebecca. I don't want trousers to look pretty on me.'

Rebecca laughed at her big brother, putting her hand to her mouth, saying, 'I forgot you're a boy.'

Then their mummy said, 'You need to hurry up, and it's okay for you to both look pretty! Take the trousers off, Jacob. Rebecca, your leggings too. They have to be paid for.'

A few minutes later, they left the changing rooms.

Jacob's mummy said to him, 'I need to buy some things for myself and your dad. Mind your little sister for me and stay close.'

'Yes, Mummy,' said Jacob. He turned to his little sister and said, 'Did you hear what Mummy said?'

'Yes,' she said. 'I'm to stay close to you, Jacob.' She continued, 'Let's play hide and seek!' and before Jacob could say no, his little sister disappeared in among the clothes rails. Jacob had his hands full. It was a hard job keeping up with her.

Every now and then, their mummy would call. The two of them would walk over and she would say something like, 'Rebecca, I hope you're behaving yourself for Jacob? Are you doing what he's telling you?'

Rebecca would say 'Yes,' and then glance at Jacob and give a little giggle.

Their mummy said, 'I will only be another few minutes. I nearly have everything. Then we'll go and pay for the clothes.' A few minutes later, she called and they queued up at the cash register and paid for the clothes. Their mummy was carrying lots of bags with shopping, so Jacob offered to help. His mummy gave Jacob the lightest bag. His guardian angel said to him, 'That's good of you to help your mummy.' Jacob just smiled to himself as he walked alongside his mummy and little sister out of the shopping centre to the car park.

When they reached the car, his mummy put all the bags on the ground. She picked up Rebecca and put her into the car. Then she opened the boot and put the shopping bags in with Jacob's help. Jacob got into the car beside his little sister and fastened his seatbelt.

A minute later, his mummy was driving out of the car park and they were on their way home. Jacob sang some songs in the car with his mummy and sister and in no time at all, they were home. His mummy parked the car outside the house in their usual spot.

Chapter 4

Where is Snuggles?

As soon as their mummy said, 'It's okay to get out of the car,' Jacob undid his seatbelt and opened his door. He hopped out and ran around to the other side of the car to where his sister was. She was so independent. She had already opened her seatbelt. Their mummy was standing at the car door with Jacob. Rebecca was insisting that she could get out of the car herself and he said, 'Remember what Mummy said. Turn around and get out backwards, and hold on to the seat.' Jacob was standing right behind his little sister and so was his mummy, just in case she slipped. They didn't want her to hurt herself.

When Rebecca was out of the car, their mummy said, 'Let me open the door.'

The two of them ran into the house while their mummy unpacked the car.

Jacob and Rebecca were helping their mummy to set the table for dinner when Jacob's guardian angel, Grasshopper, whispered in his ear, 'Your daddy will be home soon.'

Shortly thereafter, Jacob heard the key turn in the door. It *was* their dad. The two of them ran out into the hall. He picked up Rebecca first, gave her a big hug and asked if she had been a good girl today for her mummy and Jacob. She said, 'Yes.'

Then his dad said to Jacob, 'How is my little man?' He gave him a big hug and asked him what they had done during the day. Rebecca ran and got the picture that she had drawn over Jacob's picture and showed her dad. He said, 'That's lovely.' Then he smiled and gave Jacob a wink. Rebecca ran into the front room and fetched her new leggings and socks, and her daddy said, 'So you went shopping?'

Jacob said, 'Yes. We went into the big shopping centre and I got new trousers and socks as well.'

His dad said, 'Go get them and show them to me.'

As Jacob walked into the front room, his guardian angel whispered in his ear, 'Don't say anything yet, Jacob, but something is missing.'

Jacob spoke back to his guardian angel in this mind, 'Don't be silly, Grasshopper. Nothing is missing.'

He picked up his new socks and trousers and hurried back into the kitchen to show his dad, who said, 'Put them up against you and let me see. You'll look very smart in them.'

'Put them back into the front room now,' said his mummy. Jacob ran back into the front room. Grasshopper whispered to him again that something was missing, but Jacob took no notice of his guardian angel and ran over and sat beside his little sister on the couch.

A while later, their mummy said, 'Let's all sit at the table and just before I serve up the dinner, let's all say a little prayer and be thankful for all that we have today.'

Minutes later, Jacob and Rebecca clapped their hands, saying, 'Dinner was yummy.' It was spaghetti bolognese – Jacob and Rebecca's favourite. There was not a speck of food left on their plates.

Jacob helped clear the table and said, 'Thanks, Mummy, for a yummy dinner.'

She said, 'You are welcome.'

Jacob and Rebecca played games with their dad before bedtime.

Later on, Rebecca's dad said to her, 'Where are your jammies? It is time for bed.'

She ran and got them for her dad to help her put on.

A few minutes later, she was in her jammies and ready for bed, when all of a sudden, she had a very serious look on her face, and she started to cry. Through her sobs she said, 'Where is Snuggles?'

Everyone went silent for a moment and
looked at each other in horror. Rebecca
continued to cry. She was sobbing so
hard that there was no consoling her.
Jacob said, 'Snuggles must be out in the car.'

His mummy went straight out to the car and searched
it, but there was no sign of Snuggles. Rebecca would not
stop sobbing.

Their mummy said to their dad, 'Rebecca won't sleep
without Snuggles. She's heartbroken at the thought of
losing him. Maybe we left him in the shopping centre.'

Jacob added, 'Maybe in the dressing room. I remember picking Snuggles up once and sticking him in her
pocket. Maybe Snuggles fell out again later. I can't
remember.'

Jacob was now crying too because he knew his little
sister was so hurt. He was so upset for her. He ran into
the front room and searched everywhere: among the
toys, on the couch, under the pram, in every single
corner. His guardian angel was whispering to him all
the time, but he was not listening. He could only hear
the cries of his little sister back in the kitchen.

His dad suggested ringing the shopping centre, so his
mummy did so. They told her there were actually three
little fluffy rabbits found in the centre today. His

mummy asked if they could describe them to her. The first one was black in colour. The second one was a dark brown, but the other sounded a lot like Snuggles. 'Hold on to it. I'll be right there.'

'Not to worry,' said the lady. 'We'll keep it for you. Just go to reception when you arrive. It will be left there.'

Jacob's guardian angel was whispering in his ear, telling Jacob, 'Calm down. It's okay. Tell your mummy that Snuggles is here in the house.' But Jacob wasn't listening. He was hugging his little sister, trying to console her, telling her that the lady in the shopping centre believed they had Snuggles.

Jacob's mummy picked up the car keys from the kitchen table and off she went to the shopping centre. Jacob and his dad were trying to console Rebecca. Dad said, 'In no time at all, Mummy will be back, Rebecca,' as he gave her a big hug.

Jacob said, 'Don't be crying,' but no matter how hard Rebecca tried to stop, she couldn't. She just kept on sobbing as she kept on thinking of her toy bunny rabbit, who she hadn't been to sleep without since she was a little baby.

When the phone rang, Jacob's dad picked it up. It was his mummy. She was at the shopping centre. Jacob knew from the expression on his dad's face that things were not good.

The toy rabbit at the shopping centre wasn't Snuggles, and Mummy was now on the way home.

Jacob's guardian angel continued to whisper in his ear many times but Jacob still wasn't listening. Every time he looked at his little sister sitting in their dad's arms, sobbing, it made him feel very sad. Grasshopper didn't give up whispering – he knew Jacob would listen eventually.

Jacob walked sadly from the dining room out into the hall, and into the front room. He sat on the couch with his hands on his face. His guardian angel had his arms wrapped around him. Grasshopper whispered again in his ear, in a soft and gentle voice: 'Jacob, don't you remember? You picked up Snuggles for Rebecca more than once in the shopping centre. Do you remember where you eventually put him, Jacob?'

'No, Grasshopper, I don't remember.'

Jacob was only half listening to his guardian angel because he was trying to remember every step he took with his little sister in the big shopping centre.

Grasshopper whispered in his ear, 'You remember, Jacob, where you put it. It fell out of her pocket, remember, more than once.'

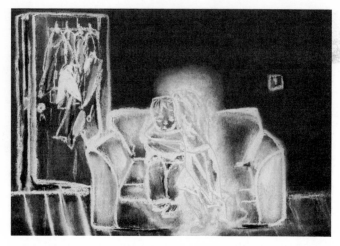

*Jacob crying on the couch with his guardian angel wrapping him
in a hug. Jacob doesn't remember that Snuggles is in the coat
pocket, hanging off the door in the background*

Suddenly, Jacob sat up on the couch and he said to his
guardian angel, in his mind, 'Yes, I remember pushing
Snuggles into Rebecca's pocket. Her pocket had no zip. I
can't remember what happened after that.'

Grasshopper whispered in Jacob's ear again, 'Remember
how you followed your sister around the shop and brought
her back to your mummy every now and then?'

Jacob shouted, 'Yes!' He put his hand to his mouth,
not meaning to shout out loud.

He spoke silently in his mind to Grasshopper as he suddenly jumped up off the couch, 'Snuggles fell out of Rebecca's pocket so many times. I was getting annoyed, but I can't remember what I did with Snuggles in the end. Did I go back over to my mummy, Grasshopper, and put Snuggles into one of the shopping bags? Maybe Snuggles is still in the shopping bags.'

The bags were standing in the corner in the front room. Jacob turned them upside down, one by one, but Snuggles wasn't there.

He spoke to Grasshopper as he sat on the floor in disappointment, with tears in his eyes, 'Grasshopper, I hate to see my little sister so sad. I have to find Snuggles for her. She will never go to bed and go to sleep again'

Jacob's guardian angel whispered in his ear, 'Don't be sad, Jacob. You haven't lost Snuggles. Look up at the door, Jacob.'

He was feeling so sad that he wasn't listening properly to his guardian angel. He didn't look up at the door. Instead, he looked all around the room. His guardian angel knew he was so upset and that was why he wasn't hearing him properly. Then his guardian angel told him, 'Everything will be all right. Snuggles is right here in this room.'

Jacob gave a sigh and said to Grasshopper, 'But where is Snuggles? I have searched the whole room and

I can't find Snuggles.' By now tears were running down Jacob's face. His guardian angel wiped away his tears and said, 'Jacob, look up at the back of the door with all the coats hanging on the door hooks.'

At that very moment, a big smile came across Jacob's face. He let out a shriek of delight. He heard the key turning in the front door. His mummy was home. He shouted, 'I remember where Snuggles is! Snuggles is right here in my coat pocket.'

Jacob climbed up onto the arm of the couch, reached up and took his coat down from the back of the door. He looked up at his mummy as she came through the door, saying 'Silly me, I forgot. I put Snuggles into my pocket because it had a zip. Snuggles kept falling out of Rebecca's pocket and I got fed up picking him up off the floor in the shop. My pocket had a zip and I knew Snuggles wouldn't fall out of my pocket!'

Rebecca was shouting, 'Snuggles!' as their dad, carrying her in his arms, rushed into the front room. There was Jacob on the floor, zipping down his coat pocket and pulling out Snuggles. He held Rebecca's little toy rabbit up to her. She lit up in her dad's arms and started to laugh with excitement.

As soon as their dad put Rebecca down on the floor, she rushed over to

Jacob and took Snuggles in her arms and hugged him tightly. 'Thank you, big brother, for finding Snuggles for me. Now I can go to bed and go to sleep.' Then she gave Jacob a big hug.

The drama was over, and when Jacob's mummy, dad and sister started to walk back into the kitchen, Jacob said to his mummy and dad, 'I'll be in in a minute. I have to tidy up the toys that I moved around looking for Snuggles.'

That was only an excuse Jacob made so he could have a little time to talk silently with his guardian angel. 'Thank you for helping me to remember where my little sister's Snuggles was. How could I manage without you? My guardian angel, Grasshopper,' said Jacob with a smile on his face.

Grasshopper whispered, 'I'm always here with you, Jacob. I never leave you for one second.'

'Thank you,' said Jacob as he walked out of the room and watched his mummy and dad go up the stairs with Rebecca. His dad was carrying her. She fell asleep in his arms, holding on to Snuggles tightly.

A little while later, they were back down. Jacob's dad read a story to him while sitting on the couch. His mummy gave him a drink and a biscuit for remembering that Snuggles was in his pocket.

'Sorry, Mummy,' said Jacob, 'that you had to go all the way into the shopping centre before I remembered putting Snuggles in my own pocket.'

'Don't worry. It was kind of funny,' said his mummy, giving him a big hug.

An hour later, Jacob went up to bed with his mummy. 'Into the bathroom first,' she said, 'and scrub those teeth. Get them snow white.'

'Yes, Mummy, I will wash my face and hands too.'

When he was finished, he said, 'All done,' to his mummy. Then, he asked her, 'Could I peep in the door of Rebecca's bedroom?'

'Go ahead. Be quiet,' she said.

He opened the door as gently and as slowly as he could, so as not to make a sound in case he woke his little sister. When he peeped in her bedroom door, he saw his little sister lying in her bed, fast asleep with Snuggles, her little toy bunny rabbit, held tight in her arms. Jacob smiled, and closed the door gently and went into his own bedroom.

He said his prayers with his mummy and afterwards asked, 'Could you leave the light on for a few minutes?'

His mummy said, 'Yes.' When she had left the room, he reached under the bed and took out his box with all his secret things in it. He took out his pencils and the paper that he'd been drawing a picture on over the last few nights when he went to bed. He drew a little bit every night. He looked at the picture – just a little more to do and then it would be finished.

Afterwards, Jacob put everything back into the box and pushed it as far as he could under his bed, but not the picture. He climbed out of bed, taking his picture in his hand, and opened his bedroom door quietly. He hoped his mummy and dad would not hear him. He opened the door of his little sister's bedroom as quietly as he could and put the picture at the end of her bed. He had drawn Snuggles for her, and he was so glad he had been able to finish the drawing that night so he could now put it at the end of Rebecca's bed as a little present.

He glanced back in at his little sister sleeping before closing her bedroom door gently. He went back to his room and turned the light off. With just the moonlight coming through the window, he climbed back into bed. He said goodnight to Grasshopper and thanked him for helping him to remember where Snuggles was, and then he fell fast asleep.

The next morning, his little sister jumped on his bed. She was holding Snuggles in one hand and the drawing of Snuggles in the other, shouting at Jacob to wake up. She gave her brother a big hug and kiss on his cheek before shouting again, 'Get out of bed, Jacob. You've got to put the picture of Snuggles on my wall over my bed so when I open my eyes, I see the picture every morning.'

'Okay,' he said.

His sister pointed out where she wanted the picture. 'Right there,' she said.

'Wait a second,' said Jacob.

He went back into his room and got the Blu Tack that his mummy had left on the top shelf for putting pictures on the wall. Jacob went back into Rebecca's room and stuck a little bit of the Blu Tack onto each corner of the drawing as Rebecca sat on her bed, pointing to the exact spot where she wanted the picture of Snuggles on her wall.

When Jacob was done, she climbed off her bed, stood back and admired the picture. 'You are the best brother in the world, Jacob.'

He said to Rebecca, 'I know I am. You are lucky, little sister, to have me as your big brother.'

The two of them ran down the stairs laughing. His mummy said, 'Toast and marmalade for breakfast, and who would like a little porridge?'

Both of them said they would love some porridge and a sice of toast. Jacob's guardian angel whispered in his

Jacob walking quietly into his little sister Rebecca's room to leave his drawing at the foot of her bed as a surprise.

ear as he sat at the kitchen table, eating his bowl of porridge, 'Today is another day full of adventures.'

Jacob replied to his guardian angel in his mind, 'I will listen better today, that I promise, Grasshopper.'

JOHNNY

Chapter 1

Can We Get a Pet?

Johnny burst through the back gate of his house and in through the back door. His mum was at the kitchen sink. She said, 'Get your homework done, Johnny.'

'Do I have to?'

'Yes, get out your books. The sooner you get your homework done, the more time you will have to play.'

He threw his schoolbag up onto the kitchen table and took out his schoolbooks. He started working on his homework as quickly as he could, but halfway through he began to daydream about having a pet. Perhaps a little black puppy with two white front paws, or maybe a kitten? Johnny gave a little sigh and said to himself as he was daydreaming that it would be fine to have a kitten. Johnny was thinking now of a tiny ball of black and white fluff. Even a goldfish in a bowl would do. He just wanted a pet of his own. He knew his birthday was coming up and every year, he hinted to his mum and dad about having a pet. They did not seem to hear him, or it fell on deaf ears.

Now his mum called, 'Johnny, stop daydreaming. Get your homework done.'

At the same moment, Johnny's guardian angel put his arms around his shoulders and whispered into his ear, 'No more daydreaming, Johnny. Do your homework.'

Johnny answered back in a quiet voice, 'Okay.' Half an hour later he was finished. He stuffed all his schoolbooks back into his schoolbag.

Just as he was about to get down from the table, his mum said to him, 'I want you to do your reading out loud for me.'

'But, Mum, I've done it already.'

She said, 'I would love to hear you read.'

His mum came over and sat down at the table. He gave a big sigh and his guardian angel whispered in his ear, 'Your mum loves you.'

So, Johnny took out his reading book and started to read for her. He read the three pages his teacher had given them for homework.

Just as he was about to finish reading, Johnny looked up at his mum and saw she was enjoying listening to him, so he continued. In another few minutes he had finished reading a whole story from his book.

'Well done,' his mum said. 'I love listening to you reading Johnny. Being read to is something I've always loved. When I was a little girl my granny would read to me.' She told Johnny of how they would sit on the couch and her granny would read for a whole hour.

'I like reading for you,' said Johnny as he jumped down from the table and gave his mum a hug. 'Can I go out to play now?'

His mum said, 'Yes.'

He ran out the back door, around the side of the house and out the front gate onto the street. His guardian angel whispered in his ear, 'Stop.' Johnny did as his guardian angel said. He stood at the edge of the footpath and he looked left and right to make sure the road was clear so he could cross over to the green where he could see his friends playing.

When it was safe, he ran across the road and joined them.

Johnny was having great fun with his friends when he heard his mum calling him for dinner. He said goodbye to his friends, and this time his guardian angel didn't have to tell Johnny to stop to make sure the road was safe before he crossed. Johnny remembered himself, and when he reached the other side, he saw his dad's car in the driveway.

Just before Johnny reached the back door, he stopped running and said to his guardian angel, 'Please let Mum and Dad say yes to a pet for my birthday present.'

Then, he opened the back door and went inside. Johnny's dad asked, 'How was your day at school?'

'It was great, and all my homework is done.'

Then Johnny and his dad played a game of boxing for a few minutes in the kitchen until his mum said, 'Stop that, you pair!'

Johnny's dad protested. It always made Johnny giggle when his dad said no to his mum. It was a fun game and Johnny loved it, but eventually his dad did listen to his mum, and they stopped. There wasn't really enough room in the kitchen for playing boxing.

'Okay,' said Johnny's dad, 'let's set the table for dinner.'

Johnny couldn't reach the cupboard where the dinner plates were, so his dad handed them to him and a few minutes later, the table was ready.

Johnny's mum started to serve up the dinner. It was chicken and vegetables – one of Johnny's favourites.

Halfway through dinner, Johnny reminded his mum and dad about his birthday in a week's time and how much he would love to have a pet of his own. 'A puppy, a kitten or a fish in a bowl.' There was silence at the table for a few moments. Johnny held his breath and then his dad said, 'Shall we all go for a walk in the forest?'

Johnny was so disappointed with his mum and dad that he ignored the question he had been asked. He told his guardian angel, Deaf Ears, that his mum and dad had deaf ears.

Johnny's guardian angel wrapped his arms around him and whispered in his ear, 'Try again. Maybe they will listen when you go for that walk in the forest with them after dinner.'

'If only you could get them to change their mind and allow me to have a pet,' said Johnny to his guardian angel in his mind as he sat at the table, looking at his mum and dad.

When dinner was over, Johnny cleared the table. His dad washed the dishes and his mum dried them.

A few minutes later, they all got into the car and drove to the forest, a twenty-minute drive from their home. Johnny loved going to the forest and so did his mum and dad. They followed different trails and Johnny climbed up onto the tree trunks, walking along the length of them and trying to keep his balance. They had lots of fun. There were lots of other mums, dads and children in the forest as well, and some of the children had dogs with them. Johnny felt a little sad when he saw them, for he desperately wanted a dog of his own.

His dad said, 'Let's sit on this tree trunk for a little

while and just look across the
pond and watch the ducks and
swans.' So, they all sat down. Deaf Ears
whispered into Johnny's ear, 'Try again.'

'Okay,' Johnny said. Taking a deep breath, he got up off
the tree trunk, and stood in front of his mum and dad and
said to them, 'Can I not have a pet for my birthday?
Wouldn't it be great fun to have a dog with us in the forest?'
Just as Johnny said this, a group of children came running
over with their dog, a black Labrador. It stood in front of
Johnny for a moment, wagging its tail, and the children
said, 'Hello!' Then they ran off and their dog ran with them.

'I would love a pet,' said Johnny. Again, his mum and
dad looked at him. At first, they didn't say a word, but
Johnny just stood there. He wasn't going to move. 'It's
my birthday, Mum, next week.'

She said, 'Johnny, you can have a party and invite all
your friends from school. And we will get you a present,
but no pets.' His dad nodded agreement with his mum.
Johnny pleaded with them, but no matter what he said,
nothing worked.

Johnny asked his mum and dad, 'Why? Why? Why?'
every time, but his mum and dad didn't answer him. He
said to them, with tears in his eyes, 'You are so mean,
and I hate you! I would love a pet of my own.'

His mum and dad laughed kindly at him and said, 'We love you,' and they put their arms around Johnny, saying again, 'We love you. You are the best little boy.' His dad continued, 'But no pets. You are not to ask again.'

Then, Johnny's dad said, 'Let's have a race to that big tree.'

Johnny said, 'I don't want to. I want to just go home now.'

His guardian angel whispered in his ear and said to Johnny, 'Race with your dad. Don't sulk. Your dad doesn't like that.'

Johnny did as his guardian angel said and started to run, shouting, 'Fooled you!'

His dad ran after him as they raced towards the big tree. The two of them reached it at the same time. They ran another three races as they headed towards the car. Johnny's mum joined in and Johnny won two of the races.

Johnny's mum drove the car home. As they were driving, his dad glanced back at Johnny and said to him, 'Take that sad face off, Johnny. I want to see you smiling.' When Johnny's dad said that to him, he remembered what his guardian angel had said earlier on – not to sulk. So, Johnny gave his dad a big smile. In fact, Johnny smiled a lot as he sat in the car on the way home because he was daydreaming of a pet of his own.

In no time at all, his mum was parking the car in the driveway. She gave him a cup of milk and a cookie while he watched TV for a little while. 'It's almost time for bed,' she eventually said. 'Go up and wash your face and hands, and clean your teeth.'

His dad said, 'I will be up to see you in a few minutes to read you a story.'

Johnny said, 'Thanks, Dad,' and ran up the stairs to get ready for bed. He shouted down the stairs to his dad that he was getting into bed and a few minutes later, his dad came up the stairs with a storybook in his hand. His dad sat on the edge of Johnny's bed, saying, 'This story is called *Huckleberry Finn*.'

Johnny said, 'That's a funny name. I've never heard a name like that before – Huckleberry Finn!' and he laughed.

'I'll read you one chapter,' Johnny's dad said as he opened the pages of the book and started to read the story to him.

His dad finished the first chapter in what seemed like just a couple of minutes, asking, 'Do you like the story so far?'

Johnny said, 'Yes, I love it. Please, could you read another chapter? Please, Dad.'

But his dad said, 'No. Now it's time for you to go to sleep,' as he kissed Johnny on the forehead. 'Don't forget to say your prayers.'

Johnny said, 'I never forget to say my prayers.'

His dad went out of the room and closed the door.

Johnny lay in bed and thanked Deaf Ears for helping him today, for reminding him not to run across the road without checking to make sure it was safe. Just as he was about to close his eyes, he said to his guardian angel, 'I would still love a pet,' and then he fell asleep.

Johnny's mum and dad gave him a great party for his birthday with his schoolfriends. They all went to the zoo and had great fun.

CHAPTER 2

A NEW FRIEND

A few weeks after Johnny's birthday, when he was walking to school, he saw a black and white cat coming towards him. The cat walked in a circle around him and then rubbed itself against his leg. He bent down to pet it. 'Hello, what's your name?' Johnny said to the cat as it purred loudly and gave a little meow. Then, as Johnny said goodbye to the cat and started again to walk to school, the cat jumped up onto the wall and began to follow him.

Johnny stopped lots of times and tried to chase the cat away, but it would only respond by jumping up and down from the wall. The cat would run away a little distance, and as soon as Johnny started to walk on, it would follow him again. It followed Johnny right to the school gate. He ran across the schoolyard and as he opened the front door, he looked back and he saw the black and white cat sitting on the pillar of the school gate.

During the break, when Johnny came out to play, he looked around to see if the cat was anywhere to be seen, but there was no sign of it. He felt relieved but also a little disappointed. He said to his guardian angel, 'Please don't let anything happen to the cat. I hope it got back home safe to whoever owns it.'

His guardian angel whispered in his ear, saying, 'Yes, it's good.'

Johnny ran off to play with his friends in the schoolyard.

After school, as Johnny walked across the schoolyard towards home, he couldn't believe his eyes when he saw the cat was on the pillar of the school gate again. All the children were reaching up to pet it. Johnny ignored it as he walked through the gate and stopped at the pedestrian crossing. He had only just got across the road when he felt something rubbing against his leg. He looked down and there again, to his surprise, was the black and white cat.

It was definitely following him. He ran and the cat ran after him. When Johnny stopped and walked, the cat stopped and walked beside him. Some of his friends came up to Johnny and said, 'Did you get the cat as a pet for your birthday?'

Johnny said, 'No, I don't really know who owns it. It followed me this morning to school.'

Johnny's friend, Tommy, said, 'And now it's following you home!'

His friends all asked if they could walk as far as the crossroads with him, because they had never known a cat to follow anyone before.

'Of course,' said Johnny.

When they reached the crossroads, he said goodbye to his friends. They all said goodbye to the black and white cat too, and the cat said goodbye to the children by rubbing up against their legs as they petted it. They shouted to Johnny, 'See you tomorrow!' as they crossed the road.

The cat then followed Johnny almost all the way home. Just before you reach Johnny's house, there is a lane leading up to another house. That is where Johnny had met the black and white cat that morning. At the entrance to this lane, the black and white cat ran around Johnny in a circle, darted up the lane and then disappeared into the garden of another house.

From then on, every morning when Johnny went to school, the cat was there to meet him in the same spot. It went all the way down to the school with him, jumping up and down off the wall, trying to get Johnny to pet it. Every time Johnny scratched it behind the ears, it purred so loudly. When he reached the school, the cat jumped up onto the pillar of the school gate and watched him go in the school door. After school, the cat was always waiting for him on the pillar of the gate.

The cat was getting a name for itself, and so was Johnny. The cat was so playful. It would jump in the air and tumble head over heels, and it always made Johnny laugh, as well as all the other children, so Johnny called it Tumbles.

CHAPTER 3

MEETING TRISH

One day, on his way home from school, when Tumbles ran around Johnny in a circle and then bounced up the lane and into the garden of the other house, Johnny's guardian angel wrapped his arms around him and whispered in his ear, 'Follow Tumbles.'

He said to his guardian angel, 'What if I get into trouble?'

'You won't,' said his guardian angel. 'Follow Tumbles.'

'Okay,' said Johnny.

When he got up to the garden gate, he saw an old lady. 'Where have you been?' she was saying to the cat.

Then, the cat ran towards Johnny as he stood at the gate. The elderly lady said to him in a gentle voice, 'Who are you?'

He replied, 'My name is Johnny. I know your cat.'

'He has been very bold for the last six weeks,' she said. 'Every morning, he goes missing for a half an hour and then, just before three o'clock, he disappears again and comes back around this time.'

Johnny said, 'That's all my fault.'

'Why?' said the elderly lady.

Johnny told her the story about meeting her cat one morning going to school and that he named her cat Tumbles. Every morning, he explained, Tumbles follows him to school and every day, when school is over, Tumbles is sitting on the pillar of the gate waiting for him. And when they reach the lane, Tumbles runs up it and into her garden.

'He likes you very much,' said the elderly lady. 'I have had him two years now and only ever called him Cat, but I do love the name Tumbles, as well. What's your name, by the way?'

'Johnny. What's yours?'

'Trish,' the elderly lady replied. 'I think Tumbles belongs to both of us.'

Johnny said, 'I better go home. My mum will be worrying.'

Trish said, 'Come another day.'

'Yes, I will.'

As Johnny walked down the lane and turned left to walk up to his own house, his guardian angel whispered in his ear, 'You have a pet now Johnny. You share Tumbles with Trish.'

Johnny said, 'Yes, I do have a pet.'

Then he jumped up and down with delight, repeating, 'Yes, I have a pet!'

He was so happy. He ran in the back door, threw his schoolbag on the table and did his homework without his mum having to tell him.

Every morning, Johnny met Tumbles going to school and every day, his cat was waiting for him on the pillar to go back home.

One day, during dinner, his mum and dad said to him, 'You seem so happy these days. Have you made a new friend in school?'

The cat, Tumbles, waiting for Johnny and his guardian angel in the the usual spot on the way to school.

Johnny's guardian angel whispered in his ear, 'Tell your mum and dad about Tumbles and Trish.'

Johnny replied to his guardian angel in his mind, 'Do you think that's a good idea?'

'Yes,' said Deaf Ears.

So, Johnny turned to his mum and dad and said, 'I met an elderly lady up the lane. Her name is Trish and her cat is called Tumbles.'

His mum and dad looked across the table at him astonished. His dad asked, 'How did you meet?'

'We want to hear everything,' said his mum.

He continued, 'One day, when I was going to school a few weeks ago, Tumbles followed me to the gates, and he's been doing it every morning since. He follows me on my way home from school as well.'

His mum said, 'I will meet you after school tomorrow.'

Johnny said, 'Don't bring the car. You better walk.'

'Okay.' So, the next day after school, his mum was standing at the far side of the road. She saw the black and white cat on the pillar of the school gate and all the children petting it. One of the mothers standing close to her said, 'That cat has been there for weeks. Isn't it so cute? Wait till you see what happens next.' But before Johnny's mum could ask the woman what she meant, the woman said, 'There's my little girl,' and she walked away.

Johnny's mum saw her son running across the school-yard and out the gate. At the same time, the cat jumped down from the pillar and started to follow him. Johnny's mum stood at the far side of the road as he waited to cross, watching the cat beside him rubbing up against his leg. She smiled with surprise when he crossed the road with the cat beside him, surrounded by all the other children.

'Hi, Mum,' said Johnny. 'This is Tumbles, the cat. He seems to like you, Mum.' Tumbles was purring next to Johnny's mum's leg.

The three of them walked home together, followed by of the other children, until they reached the cross-roads. All the children said goodbye to Johnny and his mum and petted Tumbles.

The cat jumped up onto the wall as they continued walking along the road. Every time Johnny spoke to it, the cat would meow back. Johnny was telling Tumbles that this was his mum and that she liked him. His mum was fascinated by it all. The cat was responding to Johnny's every word. Every now and then, Johnny stopped to scratch the cat behind the ears and Johnny's mum laughed at the loudness of Tumbles' purring.

When they reached the lane, Tumbles jumped down off the wall and ran up the lane and disappeared into the garden of Trish's house. Johnny's guardian angel whispered in his ear, 'Ask your mum to come up with you to meet Trish. She would love a visit.'

Johnny did as his guardian angel said. 'Mum, come up with me to meet Trish.'

His mum hesitated for a moment and then said, 'Let's go.'

When they reached the gate, there was Trish. She was doing a little gardening. As Johnny opened the gate, Trish turned around. She gave them a big welcome, saying, 'Hi there, Johnny!' She waved to them with a little trowel in her hand that she was using for her gardening. Johnny gave Trish a big smile. He loved the apron that she was wearing. It was pink with pretty flowers and frills all around the edges. He never saw his mum wear an apron like that. He had only seen them in storybooks.

He introduced his mum to Trish, who invited them in for a cup of tea. They sat at the kitchen table having tea and biscuits. Trish and his mum talked a lot, so he went out into the garden and played with Tumbles.

A little while later, his mum called him from Trish's back door and said, 'We better head home now.' So, they walked to the gate with Trish and Tumbles and closed the gate behind them. Then they walked down the lane back to their own house. Johnny looked back to see if Tumbles was following him, but he wasn't and that was okay.

From that day on, Johnny's mum and dad always asked how Tumbles was. Tumbles never went up to their house. He only lived in Trish's house. During school holidays, Johnny would go up to visit so he could play with Tumbles and help a little in Trish's garden. But every time school started, Tumbles would walk to school with Johnny, and every day he would follow him home again.

CHAPTER 4

SOMETHING IS WRONG

Johnny's guardian angel, Deaf Ears, is very tall, even taller than Johnny's dad.

One day, Johnny asked Deaf Ears, 'What kind of clothes do you wear?'

Johnny's guardian angel dresses in a beautiful green cape that flows right down to his feet. Sometimes, a little of the clothes his guardian angel wears under the green cape can be seen. They are a golden colour. And now Johnny's guardian angel allowed him to catch a glimpse of his cloak. It was just for a split second, just the corner of it.

Johnny exclaimed, 'I saw a glimpse of your guardian angel cloak!'

One day, during the summer holidays, Johnny's mum called him from the kitchen and Johnny came running down the stairs. As he opened the kitchen door, he saw Tumbles on the windowsill, tapping their window with one of his paws and meowing. Johnny looked at his mum and at the same moment, his guardian angel whispered in his ear, 'Say to your mum that something must be wrong.'

'Tumbles never comes down here, Mum,' Johnny said, just as his guardian angel told him to.

His mum said, 'You're right, Johnny. Let's go straight up to Trish's house.'

Tumbles, on the kitchen windowsill, tapping the window.
Johnny hears his guardian angel and points out to his mum that
something must be wrong

As they went out the back door, Tumbles ran ahead of them. He didn't wait for them. Johnny's guardian angel whispered again in his ear, saying, 'Run, Johnny.'

Without hesitation Johnny did exactly as his guardian

angel said, and at the same time, he said to his mum, 'Let's run!'

The two of them ran up the lane and in through the back door to the kitchen. There they found Trish sitting on the floor, leaning up against one of the chairs. Johnny's mum asked, 'What happened?'

Trish explained that she went to stand up on the little stool to get something out of the cupboard when the stool moved, and she fell backwards. 'My leg hurts,' said Trish, 'and I was afraid to try and stand up just in case I've broken something. It's not too much though.' Trish reached out and petted Tumbles. She said to Tumbles, 'You are a good cat. You went and got help!'

Johnny said, 'Tumbles was tapping his paw on the kitchen window. We knew something was wrong.'

His mum had a look at Trish's leg and saw that it was starting to swell near the ankle. She told Johnny to go and get a blanket. Then his mum called an ambulance to take her to hospital.

The ambulance arrived about twenty minutes later. Johnny's mum asked him if he would he be okay for a little while on his own so she could go to the hospital with Trish.

'That's okay, Mum. You go with Trish.'

Trish said, 'Johnny, will you look after Tumbles for me until I get home from the hospital?'

Johnny replied, 'Yes, of course I will. I love Tumbles. We will have great fun.'

His mum said to Trish, 'We will take good care of Tumbles. You are not to worry.'

Trish gave a big smile and a sigh of relief and said, 'Thank you.'

Johnny watched his mum and Trish leave in the ambulance. He played with Tumbles before putting food into the cat's dish. As Tumbles was eating his food, Johnny's guardian angel whispered in his ear and said, 'You know where Trish has the paper and paints. Why don't you paint a picture for her? I know she would love that.'

So, Johnny walked into the other room and brought the paper and paint into the kitchen and put them on the table. He took a glass from the cupboard and filled it with water and then dropped the paintbrushes into it. He also gave them a clean at the kitchen sink before bringing everything over and putting it on the table. Johnny nearly always did what his guardian angel said.

When Tumbles finished eating he jumped up onto the table. Johnny had just finished painting his first picture and told Tumbles to move out of the way as he pushed the picture to one side, saying, 'Be careful. The paint is wet.' But the next moment, there was a little breeze and the painting fell to the floor. Tumbles jumped down, chasing Johnny's picture, and started pouncing on the painting with his front paws.

Deaf Ears whispered in his ear again and said to him, 'What do you think Tumbles is doing?'

Johnny said, 'He is painting his own picture now by the looks of it.' Then he thought for a moment and said out loud, as there was no one else in the house, 'I'm starting to wonder if Tumbles is magical?'

Johnny's guardian angel said, 'I definitely think so. He is a very special cat. You know that, Johnny.'

Just then, Tumbles stopped pouncing on the picture and looked up at Johnny as if to say, 'I'm finished now. What do you think of my painting?'

Johnny bent down to pick up the painting and held it in both hands, out in front of him, admiring the painting and keeping an eye on Tumbles at the same time as the cat seemed to be waiting to hear what Johnny had to say. He smiled and said, 'Tumbles, that is a beautiful painting of your paws. They are all over the page.'

Tumbles meowed back at Johnny as if to say, 'Thank you. I'm proud of my painting.'

Johnny said, 'You should come up to my house now because I will have to go home. My dad will be home soon.'

Tumbles followed Johnny out to the gate but went no further, and when he looked back, Tumbles was standing at the gate watching him.

Tumbles pouncing on Johnny's painting for Trish.

Johnny shouted, 'I'll be back later, Tumbles.'

Johnny had only been in the house a few minutes when he heard his dad's car pulling into the driveway. He ran out and started to tell him the news about Trish hurting her leg, and that his mum was with her at the hospital. But as they walked in the back door, Johnny's dad said that his mum had given him a call and had already told him what had happened. He said to Johnny, 'The good news is no bones were broken and the doctor is letting Trish out of the hospital in a few hours, so let's make something to eat first and then we will go to pick them up.'

'Before we go to the hospital,' Johnny said, 'can I run up to see Tumbles and tell him that Trish is coming home? So he won't be worried.'

His dad said, 'It's only a cat.'

Johnny said, 'No, Tumbles is magical. That's how he can do all those funny things he does. It was Tumbles who got help for Trish, Dad – he never comes down to our house, but he was on the kitchen windowsill this morning, tapping on our window with his paws. Mum and I were surprised to see him and my guardian angel told me something must be wrong with Trish.'

Johnny's dad looked at him. 'I didn't know you believed in your guardian angel. I'm glad to hear that you do, and that you're listening.'

'Dad, of course I believe in my guardian angel. Since I was a little baby, you and Mum always say that little prayer with me to him. You know the one, Dad.'

His dad said, 'I didn't know you knew how to say the prayer on your own.'

Johnny said, 'Of course I do.'

His dad said, 'Say it for me.'

'Okay,' said Johnny, and he recited the prayer:

Guardian Angel, thank you for watching over me today.
I am only a little child.

I know you are there, even though I cannot see.
I know you are always whispering in my ear
    telling me to be good.
I know you are always with me, so I am
    never ever alone.
I know that you love me, and I love you,
    my guardian angel.

'I like saying it with you and Mum at night before I go to sleep,' said Johnny. 'I don't *always* listen though, and when I don't listen, I always find I get into trouble. Sometimes I just forget though.'

Johnny's dad gave him a big hug and said, 'I am very proud of you.'

'What about Tumbles?' asked Johnny.

His dad said, 'Yes, you can go tell him Trish will be home soon. What a good cat he is, getting help for Trish.' Then Johnny's dad looked around the kitchen. 'But first, let's do some scrambled egg and toast for dinner.'

'What about some beans as well? I am really hungry,' said Johnny.

Ten minutes later, they were sitting at the table when the phone rang. Johnny's dad answered it, and as he walked back to the table he said to Johnny, 'We can go in now and collect Trish and your mum. The doctors said

Trish can go home. Don't stuff your mouth with your food, Johnny. We have plenty of time.'

Johnny said, 'But Dad, I have to run up to Tumbles first. Can you clear off the table? I will only be a minute.'

His dad said, 'Okay, off you go.'

Johnny ran up to Trish's house and in the back door, and there was Tumbles sitting on Trish's chair. Tumbles jumped off the chair as soon as Johnny came through the back door. Johnny bent down, petted Tumbles and said, 'Trish is going to be home soon. I'm going to collect her from the hospital with my dad.'

Johnny said goodbye to Tumbles and ran out the door and back down the lane. He glanced back once but he didn't see Tumbles standing at the gate, so he guessed the cat had stayed in the kitchen and didn't follow him out through the little cat flap that Trish had put in the bottom of her back door.

His dad was already in the car at the end of the lane, waiting for him.

'Let's go,' said Johnny to his dad as he got into the car and fastened his seatbelt.

Half an hour or so later, they arrived at the hospital. Trish and Johnny's mum were waiting for them in the waiting room. Trish's leg was wrapped in bandages. She had a walking stick. Johnny's dad and mum were talking with Trish. She was to keep weight off her leg as much as possible for the next week. Johnny's dad said he would go and get the car and drive it up to the main entrance.

A few minutes later, he picked them up at the main entrance of the hospital.

When Johnny was sitting in the back of the car with Trish, she said, 'Thank you, Johnny, for all your help and for looking after Tumbles for me. What would I do without you both?'

Johnny said, 'You're welcome. I love Tumbles and I love you too, Trish.'

Johnny's dad drove up to Trish's house and turned the car around. Trish and Johnny's mum got out of the car. Johnny asked, 'Can I come too?'

But his dad said, 'No, you come home with me. Your mum will only be a little while.'

That night, when Johnny went to bed, he said the guardian angel prayer that he always said at night. He said it with his dad but when his dad had left the room, he also asked his guardian angel to look after Tumbles and Trish, and not to allow Trish to have any more accidents.

'And by the way, Deaf Ears, could you ask Trish's guardian angel to please not let her fall again? And Deaf Ears, thank you again for my wonderful pet, Tumbles.'

Johnny's guardian angel whispered in his ear, 'You and Tumbles are going to have many adventures together.'

And with that, Johnny turned on his side and fell asleep, dreaming of Tumbles, his magical cat, and himself having wonderful adventures together.

TOMMY

The sun was shining through a gap in the curtains of Tommy's window. His guardian angel, whom he called Left Foot, was blowing on his face, saying, 'Tommy, open your eyes. The sun is shining. It's time to get up.'

Tommy opened his eyes and said, 'Left Foot, you remembered to wake me up so we can play football!' as he jumped out of the bed and put his clothes on. 'Where are my shoes, Left Foot?'

'Under your bed,' said his guardian angel.

As Tommy put his shoes on, he said to Left Foot, 'You know, I'm not really very good at playing football and it makes me feel very sad. My friends never let me play with them because I'm not much good at it . . . but I really do try hard.'

Tommy's guardian angel put his arms lovingly around Tommy's shoulders and whispered into his ear, 'They will ask you soon, maybe today. You are getting good at football, and I will keep helping you.'

Tommy said to his guardian angel, 'Do you really think so? Do you really think I'm getting better at football? It's only because of you, Left Foot. I would have no one to play football with, if I didn't have you.'

Left Foot said, 'Let's go and play.'

Tommy jumped off his bed and ran out his bedroom door.

His mum called out, 'Tommy, brush your teeth first, and wash your face, before coming downstairs.'

'Okay!' said Tommy as he stopped at the top of the stairs. He went back to the bathroom and stood at the sink to brush his teeth. Looking into the bathroom mirror, he made faces at himself.

Tommy's guardian angel, Left Foot, was very tall. He towered over Tommy and was dressed in the colours of Tommy's favourite football team.

Tommy came down the stairs and called out to his mum, 'Where is my football?' as he began rummaging under the stairs, firing everything out into the hall. He flung out storybooks, pencils, cars, trucks, diggers, and even his sister's dolls. He could not see his ball anywhere. He called out again: 'Mum! Where's my football?'

His mum walked over and said, 'What's going on here? What a mess!'

Tommy looked at his mum, trying not to cry. 'Sorry Mum, I was looking for my football and I can't find it.'

'Tidy up that mess, Tommy. Put everything back under the stairs. What do you want for breakfast?'

'Nothing,' he said, 'just my football.'

His mum laughed, saying as she went into the kitchen, 'Tommy, you can't eat your football for breakfast. I'll make you toast and cheese. Afterwards, I will help you look for your football.'

Tommy stood in the hall looking at all the toys on the floor. It looked like such a big job to put them all back under the stairs by himself, so he asked Left Foot to help. His guardian angel told Tommy to get the sweeping brush. Tommy said, 'What a great idea!' as he threw his hands up in the air and ran into the kitchen. He grabbed the brush, which was standing in the corner, and ran back out into the hall.

Tommy said out loud as he was sweeping all the toys back under the stairs, 'You are the best, Left Foot, you always have great ideas!'

Tommy's guardian angel said to him, 'You missed something,' as he pointed to his little sister's doll on the floor.

'Thanks, Left Foot.' Tommy manoeuvred the sweeping brush around the doll and pushed it under the stairs. He then closed the door with a big smile on his face and went back into the kitchen with the brush.

Tommy sat down at the table, drank his milk, and ate the toast and cheese as quickly as he could. As soon as he had swallowed the last mouthful of toast he said, 'Mummy, help me find my football.'

His mum said, 'No, you will have to wait until your little sister has finished her breakfast.' Tommy was disappointed. He got down from the table and went back out into the hall and sat on the stairs. He really wanted to go and practise his football.

Left Foot sat on the stairs with him, as his guardian angel always goes everywhere with Tommy, never leaves him for one second. Now Left Foot whispered into Tommy's ear, 'Maybe your football is in the front room behind the sofa?'

'Yes,' said Tommy to his guardian angel, 'I remember, I was in the front room with my football and Mummy gave out to me, but Left Foot, I can't remember where I put my football.'

'Did you not hear me? Behind the sofa, Tommy.'

Tommy sat on the stairs, pondering for another few minutes. Left Foot was constantly whispering into his ear, telling him to go into the front room and look behind the sofa. All of a sudden Tommy jumped up off the stairs and said, 'I remember! It is behind the sofa.'

'About time,' said Left Foot as Tommy jumped up, ran to the front room and opened the door.

He went behind the sofa. 'Yip! Yip!' he said. 'Thanks, Left Foot.'

Tommy leaning over the couch, looking for his football.

Tommy peeped around the door of the kitchen. Mummy was drinking a cup of tea and his little sister Katie was still eating her breakfast. 'Mummy, I found my football. Can I go out to play?'

'Where did you find it?' asked Tommy's mummy.

'Behind the sofa,' said Tommy.

'A good hiding place,' said his mum. 'Yes, you can go out to play, but only on the green.'

Tommy went out the front door and started kicking his football straight away as they went out the garden gates. Tommy said, 'Left Foot, I really need to practise. I hope the other boys will let me play with them when I get down to the green.' Tommy was really worried that he wouldn't be good enough.

Left Foot said to him, 'Kick your ball against the garden wall for a few minutes.'

'Mum might give out,' said Tommy.

'Only when you kick your ball in the house,' said Left Foot. 'Your mum knows how much you love to play football and she wants you to be able to play in the local team because she knows that will make you happy.'

'Okay,' said Tommy and he started to kick the football against the wall. Left Foot mimicked every kick Tommy made, giving him confidence.

'You're getting better with every kick!' he said.

Tommy asked, 'Do you really think so?'

'Yes,' replied his guardian angel.

After about fifteen minutes of kicking the football

against the garden wall, Tommy decided it was time to go down the lane to the green. He bounced his ball as he walked along and sometimes gave it a few kicks.

Left Foot said, 'Do your best to keep control of the ball.'

'How do you think I'm doing?' asked Tommy.

'Great,' said Left Foot.

When they got down to the green where the football pitches were, there were no other boys playing football. Tommy felt sad.

Left Foot said, 'Don't be sad, Tommy. Let's practise kicking the ball around the pitch. Every now and then, try to kick it into the goal.' When Tommy is playing football, he seems to be able to hear his guardian angel very clearly.

So, Tommy started to play football with his guardian angel, running around the field, kicking the ball, keeping it under control, and every now and then, when Left Foot said, 'Kick for the goal post.' Tommy did.

The first and second time Tommy shot at the goal, he missed. 'What's the point?' said Tommy, 'I'm no good!'

'Don't give up,' said Left Foot, encouragingly. 'Just concentrate. Kick the ball around the field and I will tell you when to shoot. When I do, make sure you really concentrate.'

Tommy hesitated for a moment, not sure whether to try again. But Left Foot encouraged him again, saying, 'Come on Tommy!'

Tommy started to kick the ball around the field, enjoying himself, and when Left Foot told him to aim for the goal, Tommy concentrated hard, and kicked.

The ball went straight into the goal. 'Yes!' said Tommy as he jumped up and down. 'That was great!'

Left Foot said, 'Now you know you can do it.'

'Yes,' said Tommy. 'Thanks, Left Foot.'

Just as Tommy started to kick the ball again, a group of boys came running over asking, 'Can we play football with you?' Tommy was astonished, because this was the first time that other boys had ever asked if they could play with him.

'Yes!' said Tommy.

Four of the boys were friends who played for the local football team. Their names were John, Paul, Simon and Mark. He had never met the other two boys before. One of his friends, Paul, said, 'This is Billy-Bob and Céadan.'

Paul said, 'Let's make two small teams for practice. Three on one side and four on the other. I pick first,' said Paul. 'I want Simon, Billy-Bob and Céadan.' John went with Mark and Tommy. 'It's a bit uneven,' said Paul, 'but that won't matter.'

Tommy's guardian angel whispered to him, 'Say to Paul, can Céadan be the goalkeeper.' Tommy was very apprehensive, but Left Foot whispered in his ear again.

Tommy plucked up the courage and said it: 'Can Céadan be the goalkeeper?'

To Tommy's surprise, Paul said, 'That's a good idea!'

They started to play football, and everything was going really well. Tommy was enjoying himself. All the boys were having great fun.

Suddenly, Tommy fell. The other boys were so engrossed in the football game that they didn't notice. Tommy sat on the ground, rubbing his leg, and when he looked up, he saw the other boys were at the far end of the pitch still playing football.

Tommy started to cry. Left Foot rubbed Tommy's leg and whispered, 'You can't give up now. You've been practising so hard for months and you have got so good at football. Get up and your leg will be fine. Don't let the other boys see you were crying. Get up, Tommy. Remember I'm playing football with you. I'm your guardian angel and I will kick the ball with you. As always.'

'Do you promise?'

'Yes,' said Left Foot. 'Now, get up.'

Tommy on the ground with his guardian angel,
Left Foot, after falling playing football.

Just as Tommy stood up, the other boys called out from the far end the pitch: 'You okay?'

Tommy shouted, 'Yes!' as he ran towards them.

Just then, Paul kicked the ball in Tommy's direction. Even though his leg was still hurting a little bit, Tommy ran towards the ball. He was determined to give it a really hard kick. Remembering what his guardian angel had said, he concentrated and struck the ball perfectly. For a fleeting second, as Tommy kicked the ball, he saw the foot of his guardian angel too, wearing boots of gold with black laces. Tommy had great fun that day, and on his way back home, he was bouncing and kicking his ball full of confidence, knowing now he could play football just like the other boys. He said to Left Foot, 'Thank you for helping me to kick the ball so well!'

Left Foot said, 'I did not kick it, Tommy, you did. My foot only went alongside the ball. I didn't even touch it.

'Thank you for letting me get a glimpse of you, even though it was only your foot,' said Tommy. He fell silent for a moment as he carried his football, thinking to himself about his guardian angel and seeing his left foot.

Tommy stopped at the gate of the house saying, 'You are my best friend, Left Foot. I don't think I will ever forget about those amazing gold football boots with their black laces.'

Tommy's guardian angel looked down at him, full of love, as Tommy opened the gate. He called to his mum to tell her all about playing football with his friends, and that super kick that showed his friends that he was as good a footballer as them.

Left Foot knows that at times Tommy may forget about him, but that doesn't matter to his guardian angel. Left Foot loves Tommy unconditionally and will never leave him for one moment. Tommy will never be alone. Left Foot will always be whispering in Tommy's ear to give him confidence and belief in himself.

Remember, you have a guardian angel, just like Left Foot. Ask your guardian angel to help you in all the things you do. Your guardian angel is your best friend and is always there with you, even when you are sleeping. Whether you are being good or bold, your guardian angel is always with you!

Tommy's guardian angel, Left Foot, teaching Tommy
to kick the football. Tommy can see the foot of
his guardian angel; kicking the ball with him.

SUZY

Suzy's dad carried her out to the car in his arms and strapped her into her car seat. Suzy's guardian angel whispered in her ear, telling her they were going on a picnic. She lit up with excitement. 'Please ask God, Peawee, for the sun to keep shining!' she said in her mind to her guardian angel. 'Why didn't Mum and Dad tell me we were going on the picnic?'

Suzy's guardian angel said, 'Because they were worried it might rain, and that you'd be disappointed. They know how you love to sit in your wheelchair, watching children playing, and all the birds and the dogs running around.'

'Okay, Peawee, I'll pretend I don't know.'

Suzy sat quietly in the car. She knew her mum was putting something into the boot of the car, but she was not able to turn around to look. Suzy's dad called out to her mum, saying, 'Make sure you push that bag to the right, so that Suzy's wheelchair can fit in.'

Suzy's sister, Megan, climbed into the car next to her and put her seatbelt on. Megan said to Suzy, 'We're going on a picnic. First, we have to pick Granny up because she's coming with us too!'

Suzy was so excited. She loved going on picnics. She gave her sister a big smile. Suzy said to herself, 'So that bag they put in the boot was a picnic basket. Mum and Dad can't keep secrets like that from me because my guardian angel tells me everything!' She said to her guardian angel, 'Should I tell my mum and dad about you?' Peawee just gave Suzy a big hug in response.

It was just a few minutes' drive to Suzy's granny's house. As they pulled up to the gates, the hall door opened and out came Suzy's granny, carrying a blanket and another picnic basket. Her dad put them into the boot. As her granny got into the car, she said to Suzy and Megan, 'I have a storybook in my bag. Would you like me to read to you two girls while Daddy is driving to the park?'

'Yes, please!' said Megan. So, their granny started a story about a little girl and a skipping rope.

Forty minutes later they drove through the park gates and into the car park. Everyone got out of the car except for Suzy. She had to wait for her dad to get her wheelchair out of the boot of the car, and then for him to unstrap her from her car seat and put her into the chair.

Within a few minutes, Suzy was sitting in her wheelchair. Her dad was carrying two picnic baskets and

Granny's blanket. Her mum was pushing Suzy in her chair.

It was a lovely day and the sun was shining. Suzy could feel the heat on her face. Her dad said, 'Let's stop here. This is a nice spot for a picnic.' Her mum put the brakes on the wheelchair, so it wouldn't move. Suzy sat there, watching everything that was going on. Her sister Megan took no time at all making friends with some other children, who were on picnics with their families too.

Suzy's mum and granny were sorting out everything for the picnic on the blankets. Suzy smiled because every now and then, part of the blanket would blow in the wind and her gran would reach out and fix it. She said to Suzy's mum, 'Give me a bottle to keep the corner of the blanket down, so the wind won't blow it away before we're all sitting down.' That was one thing Suzy loved about their picnics. The wind would blow the blankets, and scatter the paper cups and plates, and her granny would let out a little scream while trying to catch everything. It just looked so funny to Suzy.

She continued to sit in her wheelchair with a smile on her face, wishing she could get up, run around and play games just like her sister, Megan, and those other little girls and boys. Her body would give little movements as she imagined herself playing.

Suzy was watching everything that was going on. She imagined herself playing and doing all the things the other children were doing.

Suzy's body was twisted, and she was extremely thin. She was only ten years of age. With little tears running down her cheek, she said to herself, 'Why am I in a wheelchair? It's not fair.' She said this in her own mind and her guardian angel heard her. Suzy's guardian angel always heard every word. She would talk to herself in her mind because she could not talk like other girls and boys. Only her guardian angel would hear what she was saying.

Now Suzy's guardian angel knelt down beside her wheelchair and looked straight into her eyes. Suzy gave a big smile and said, 'There you are!'

'Yes, I am here,' said Peawee. 'Don't you know, I never leave you.'

'Yes, I do,' said Suzy. "I love you, Peawee.'

On very special occasions, Suzy could see as well as hear her guardian angel, and this was one of those special times. She said to her guardian angel, 'I wish I could touch your face. You are so beautiful, Peawee.'

Suzy's guardian angel had long, wavy, golden hair. Her face was radiant, and her eyes sparkled like stars.

Suzy loved to look into her guardian angel's eyes. They filled her with love.

'Don't cry,' said Peawee.

'I would love to be able to play on the grass and run around like my sister, Megan.'

'I know you would,' said Peawee.

'Please! *Please*!' said Suzy as she looked into her guardian angel's eyes.

'Okay,' said Peawee. 'You are going to sleep now, Suzy.' Peawee's left hand reached out. Radiant light streamed from her fingertips as Peawee touched Suzy's eyes, which started to close slowly as she looked into her guardian angel's eyes with a smile on her face.

Just then, Suzy's mum walked over to her, and said to her granny, 'Suzy has fallen asleep.' Her mum put a blanket around her to keep her warm. Then her mum went back and sat on the blankets, helping her granny sort the food for the picnic, chatting and enjoying the day.

Unknown to Suzy's family, something wonderful was happening to her.

As soon as Suzy was in a deep sleep, her guardian angel, ever so gently and lovingly, lifted her soul out of her body. Suzy's soul was radiant. As she left her little body asleep in the wheelchair, Suzy was a beautiful girl, perfect in every way – the way she will look when she goes home to heaven.

At the same time, four other angels appeared, two on either side of Suzy's wheelchair. The angels reached out and took Suzy's hands, walking a little distance from the wheelchair, but not very far. They were all girls, all the same age as Suzy, and were dressed in glowing white dresses that fell down to their toes, with a red ribbon tied around their waists and a bow at the back. They did not wear any shoes.

The angels were holding hands with Suzy in a circle and began playing ring-a-ring o' roses. Suzy was laughing and singing with them. Then they played chasing games, running around Suzy's wheelchair. Suzy laughed every time she touched one of the angels, because every time she did, they seemed to get brighter.

When they stopped chasing one another, the four girl angels stood around Suzy in a circle. Suzy's guardian angel said to her, 'I will have to wake you up from your sleep now.'

Suzy's soul turned around and looked at her body in the wheelchair. 'I would love to sit in the grass for a little while longer.'

Her guardian angel said, 'Okay, just for a few moments more.'

Suzy and the four angels now sat in a circle on the

The two angels on either side of Suzy pulling her soul
from her wheelchair to play.

grass, with Suzy right in front of her wheelchair. She was enjoying herself so much. Each time one of the angels touched a blade of grass with the tips of their fingers, the blade turned into a beautiful daisy.

Suzy's soul cried out with delight: 'Let's make a daisy chain!' The four angels started to make daisy chains. One of them showed Suzy how to make a daisy chain by putting little slits in the stem and putting another daisy through it. No matter how many daisies the angels picked, more seemed to appear within the circle. It was like a bed of beautiful daisies.

As the angels talked and laughed with Suzy, like little girls themselves, they put a crown of daisies on her head like a little princess, and daisy chains around her neck. Suzy quickly became very good at making the daisy chains. She put one she had made around her own wrist and then two of the angels put daisy chains around both of her ankles. Suzy admired all the daisy chains that the four little girl angels had made for her.

Daisies strung together for the daisy chains.

She thanked them and said, 'I'm having a wonderful time. I love daisy chains!'

Again, Suzy's mum looked over at Suzy asleep in her wheelchair. She didn't notice anything. She did not even notice the little smile on Suzy's face as she slept.

Suzy said to the little girl angels who were playing with her, 'What are your names?' The angels only gave Suzy a smile and put their fingers to their lips. Suzy understood that they weren't going to tell her their names and that was okay. She was so happy. She said to them, 'I watch my sister Megan and her friends making daisy chains every summer and I always wished I could do that too. Thank you!' The angels started to sing a song and Suzy sang along with them. Suzy was radiant. She was so happy and full of joy, and so were the angels.

The four angels stood up on their bare feet in their beautiful white dresses, with the red ribbon tied around the waist, and they danced around Suzy's soul in a circle, and then each angel, one by one, knelt down in front of Suzy's soul and gave her a big hug and said they loved her 'We have to go now,' they said.

Then Suzy's guardian angel Peawee lifted her soul ever so gently and carried it back to her wheelchair. She laid her soul down lovingly as it snuggled back into her human body.

Suzy surrounded by her guardian angel's wings as Peawee carries
her soul. Suzy has daisies in her hair and around her neck

A few minutes later, when Suzy opened her eyes, her
guardian angel was kneeling down at the side of her
wheelchair looking into her eyes. Suzy gave Peawee a big
smile as she spoke to her guardian angel in her mind,
saying, 'Thank you! That was great fun. Do I still have
the daisy chains on me?'

Her guardian angel said, 'Yes, but no one else can see
them, only you.' It wasn't very easy for Suzy to move but

she looked down at her wrists and she found she could see the daisy chain she had made herself.

Just then her mum called out, saying, 'You're awake, Suzy!' Her mum got up and walked over and pushed her wheelchair to where the picnic was happening. For a brief moment, when Suzy was having a drink, she saw the four little girl angels again. They were waving to her, and then they disappeared.

Suzy wanted to tell her mum all about the angels, about making the daisy chains, about playing ring-a-ring-a-roses and chasing around her wheelchair, but she couldn't. So she pretended instead that she was talking out loud with her mum and dad and her sister and her granny, and telling them what had happened, and she began to laugh out loud.

Megan said, 'Mum, Suzy is laughing again at nothing.'

Her mum asked Suzy, 'What are you laughing at? What is so funny? What's going on inside your head?'

If only her mum knew that, for a little while, when Suzy was asleep, her soul had been playing with four little angels, making daisy chains, laughing and full of joy.

Emma

CHAPTER 1

SCHOOLTIME

Emma was eight years of age and she lived out in the country. She walked to school every day. Her school was made up of small prefab buildings with three classrooms in total, plus an office and a couple of outdoor toilets. The toilets were in a little stone shed with a tin roof and a wooden partition in the middle – one side for the boys and one side for the girls. The floors were concrete and there were two washbasins. It was freezing in the toilets, especially in the wintertime.

One day, when Emma was in class, she asked her teacher if she could go out to the toilet.

Her teacher said, 'Yes, but do put on your coat.'

Emma said, 'Thank you,' as she got up from the desk and walked towards the door, where all the coats were hanging. She put her coat on, walked into the little porch, opened the door, and – when the cold breeze hit her – gave a little shiver. She closed the door behind her and walked down the three steps.

As she crossed the schoolyard, her guardian angel whispered in her ear, 'Run, Emma.'

'Why?' Emma said out loud, as she continued walking.

Her guardian angel whispered back, 'You better run. It's going to rain.'

All of a sudden, the sky darkened, and the clouds burst open. It started to lash down with rain. Emma ran across the schoolyard and straight into the toilets. She could hardly see; it was so dark because there were no windows to let light in. Emma patted her hand on the wall, just inside the door, feeling for the light switch, and turned it on.

She spoke out loud to her guardian angel, knowing that there was no one there to hear her. 'Thank you, Guardian Angel.'

Emma's guardian angel didn't reply. When Emma was finished, she washed her hands. The rain seemed to have become louder. It was pelting down on the tin roof. She walked to the door and looked out. She couldn't believe it. The schoolyard looked like a river. She spoke out loud again to her guardian angel, saying, 'I'm going to get drowned if I try to go back to my classroom! Maybe I should just stay here, but I'm freezing, and my coat is already wet.'

Emma's guardian angel whispered in her ear, 'When I say run, Emma . . . run.'

Emma's guardian angel trying to protect her from the heavy rain as she runs across the school yard.

Emma said, 'Okay but are you sure? The rain seems to be getting heavier.' She reached up to turn off the light, and stood poised in the doorway.

As soon as her guardian angel said 'Run' Emma sprinted across the schoolyard. It was like a river, and each step splashed water everywhere. Instantly Emma's feet were soaking wet, but she just kept running as fast as she could. She ran up the few steps of the little building that housed her classroom, opened the door and, once inside, closed it as quickly as she could with both hands.

As Emma pushed down on the handle of her classroom door, she spoke to her guardian angel, silently: 'My teacher is going to give out to me for getting so wet.'

'Don't worry,' said her guardian angel, 'Ms Julia won't give out to you. It wasn't your fault.'

'It was raining so heavily, really' said Emma, but her guardian angel didn't whisper back to her, so Emma took a few steps into the classroom, and proceeded to take her coat off and give it a shake. It was dripping wet, making a puddle on the floor. She, herself, looked like a drowned rat.

Ms Julia walked over to Emma with a towel in her hand, and said, 'Oh, Emma, you poor thing! Your hair is soaking wet. At least your coat kept the rest of you dry.' As her teacher took her coat from her, and dropped it on the floor, she said to Emma, 'Dry your face.'

After Emma finished drying her face, Ms Julia took the towel from her and started to dry her hair as much as she could. Two minutes later, Ms Julia said to Emma, as she stood back and looked her, 'Now, Emma, you look a little bit more respectable, not like a drowned rat.' The other children in the classroom laughed and clapped their hands.

Ms Julia told Emma to go and sit down. As she walked towards her desk, everyone could hear the squeaking coming from her shoes and see the little puddles of water left behind with each step as she crossed the classroom floor. Ms Julia called out: 'Stop, Emma; I didn't realise your feet were so wet.'

'I didn't realise my shoes were so wet,' she said. 'I can't stop my shoes from squeaking. Sorry, Ms Julia,' said Emma.

'Take off your shoes,' said Ms Julia.

As Emma took her shoes and socks off, her teacher went over to one of the cabinets and took out a pair of socks and an old pair of slippers for Emma to put on her feet. 'Thank you,' she said to her teacher.

'You are welcome, Emma. Go and sit down.'

Ms Julia picked Emma's shoes up off the floor and stuffed them with some newspaper. She said, 'I hope they will be dry enough for you, Emma, by the time school is over.' Then, Ms Julia picked Emma's socks up and wrung them out over the bin, as there was no sink in the classroom. After that, she picked the soaking wet coat up off the floor, leaving a huge puddle of water there. The coat trailed water across the floor as Ms Julia carried it across the room and hung it on the back of a spare chair, putting some newspaper on the floor just under Emma's coat so it wouldn't get too wet. This didn't seem to really work. There was just too much water.

As they watched the newspaper soaking up the water, one of the other children sitting at their desks said to the teacher, 'Ms Julia, you're going to need a lot of newspaper.'

One of the other little girls, called Annamarie, now put her hand up and said, 'Ms Julia, I know where there are some more newspapers.'

As Ms Julia mopped up the water dripping from Emma's coat with the few newspapers she had, she said, 'Go get them, Annamarie.'

Annamarie got up from her desk, ran over to where the coats were hanging, and pulled out a box. She dragged it over towards her teacher, and said, 'This is full of newspapers. Our teacher last year had us all bring in any newspapers our mums and dads didn't want.'

'Thanks, Annamarie,' said Ms Julia. 'Now, go back to your desk.'

One of the boys in the class, called Martin, ran to the back of the teacher's desk to get the bin. Then he helped Ms Julia put the wet paper into it.

A few minutes later, Ms Julia stood up and said to Martin, 'Thank you, job well done. Now go sit down.'

Ms Julia looked over to the coat hanging on the back of the chair. 'It is still dripping water on the floor,' she said, 'But I think we have enough newspapers.' She gave a sigh of relief.

Sitting back at her desk, Emma spoke to her guardian angel in her mind: 'I like this teacher, Ms Julia.' Emma's guardian angel didn't reply, so she continued: 'Ms Julia is a new teacher at our school. Did you know that my guardian angel?' But, again, her guardian angel didn't answer her, so she continued again: 'The oldest teacher in the school retired. Her name was Ms June. Ms Julia is so nice and kind. She didn't give out to me for getting soaking wet in the rain. Ms Julia is teaching three classes: second, third and fourth class.'

Between the three year groups, who all shared the classroom, Ms Julia was teaching only sixteen children.

Emma's guardian angel whispered in her ear to pay attention: 'Your teacher is sitting back at her desk. She's going to give you some work to do, Emma.'

Ms Julia was getting up from her desk and spoke to the fourth class: 'Please take out your geography text-book. I want you to do pages ten and eleven.' Then, Ms Julia walked over to the first row of children – Emma's row – which was where the fourth class sat.

Emma was very bright, and she finished both pages in no time at all. She always listened to what her teacher said to the other classes, but sometimes the girl behind her would distract her by tapping on her shoulder with a pencil, asking her to help with one of the questions. The two girls had whispered to each other the first few times this happened and Ms Julia gave out to the two girls in the beginning, but over time, she realised that Emma's work was always correct and she was only helping the girl behind her. This time Ms Julia didn't say a word, but *did* give them a look. Emma whispered to her friend behind her, explaining what the question meant, and then turned back around.

Light started to shine in the window and Ms Julia said, 'The sun has come out just in time for your lunch break. If you have sandwiches or a drink, eat them now in the classroom. If you have fruit, you can take that out into the yard with you.'

Everyone sat at their desks and ate their sandwiches.

A few minutes later, the children started to get up to go out into the yard and play.

Sometimes Emma could be a bit of a brat. When this happened, her guardian angel would tell her that what she was doing was mean and unfair, and how would she like if someone else did those things to her, but a lot of the time, Emma did not listen to her guardian angel. And today, during lunch break, while playing hopscotch in the schoolyard, Emma was being mean to some of her friends.

As they were playing, one of her friends, Mary, said to Emma, 'That's not fair. It's my turn now.'

Emma's guardian angel was whispering in her ear: 'Don't be a brat, Emma. Be fair.'

But Emma spoke back to her guardian angel in her mind, saying, 'I'm the boss here,' and stamping her foot. Mary stepped back nervously when Emma did this, not knowing that she was stamping her foot at her guardian angel.

As Mary stood there, Emma just raised her eyebrows and said to Mary, 'No, for saying that, you're not playing anymore.'

So now Mary stood to one side, waiting for Emma to get over her strop and let her back into the game – which is what usually happened when Emma insisted on having her way.

This time, the game was almost over before, finally, Emma listened to her guardian angel and allowed Mary back into the game. Mary had only one turn just before the bell rang and they all ran back into class.

Just a few minutes before school was over, Ms Julia asked the class, 'Have there ever been any activities after school hours here?'

One of the children said, 'No, what do you mean?'

'Like art, drama or dancing?'

'No, we've never had anything like that,' said another of the children.

The next moment, the bell rang, and Ms Julia said to her pupils, 'Those that are walking home, be careful, and those that are waiting on a lift, don't leave the schoolyard till your parents get here.'

All the children said, 'Yes, Teacher.'

Then Ms Julia said, 'See you in the morning!'

Gradually, all the children left the classroom with their schoolbags and coats. The sun was still shining.

Ms Julia was finished tidying her things up in the classroom when her guardian angel whispered in her

ear to go and talk to the two other
members of staff, one of whom was
the principal, and to ask them about
what was on her mind.

She did exactly as her guardian angel said. She took
her coat and bag, and locked the classroom door, before
walking over to one of the other prefab buildings. It was
the smallest of them all and functioned as the office. The
other two teachers were there, getting ready to leave.

Ms Julia said, 'Could I have a word?'

'Yes,' said the principal.

The three of them sat down around the principal's
desk. The principal's name was Martha and the other
teacher's name was Marion. Julia said to them, 'I've
been here now a few months, and I have noticed that the
children don't seem to have any activities after school.'

Principal Martha said, 'No one wants to come out to a
little school with such small numbers of children. It's not
worthwhile for them, and money is an issue. Drama teachers are expensive, and so are art teachers, and even dancing. With the number of children here, they wouldn't make
enough money, so they don't see it as being worthwhile.'

There was silence for a moment and Ms Julia felt
disappointed, but just then her guardian angel whispered in her ear to give her confidence: 'Say it.'

Ms Julia said, 'I am a qualified dancing teacher.'

The principal looked at her in surprise and said, 'What? You never put that on your CV.'

'No, because I never thought it would be of any benefit in the school. I taught dancing for a few years, and then went on to qualify as a primary school teacher. I could give dancing lessons after school.'

The other teacher, Marion, said, 'That would be absolutely marvellous! Maybe at the end of the year the children could even do a little dance show.'

The principal said, 'You're not going to make any money out of this, Ms Julia.'

'That's okay,' Ms Julia said, 'I'll do it for free. But how about we ask the children for one euro each, once a week, and that would help for other things needed in school.'

The other teachers thought this was a great idea, but the principal had to first see what insurance cover the school had. 'We should know by the end of the week,' Principal Martha said, while packing things into her case.

The principal and the two teachers left the office. As they were walking across the playground and out the school gate, they said goodbye to each other, got into their cars and drove away.

Chapter 2

Painting the Shed Door

Every day, when Emma got home from school, she would give her mum a helping hand with her two little twin brothers, Johnny and Paul. They were three years of age, and they were a handful. Sometimes Emma called them little brats, but she loved them.

The two little boys loved their big sister too. She would push them on the swing and play football with them when her mum was doing other things in the house. Sometimes, though, Emma would get up to mischief, even though she was eight years of age and knew better. Her guardian angel was always whispering in her ear asking her to be good but sometimes she would get her little brothers into trouble.

One day, her dad brought home a tin of paint and some new paintbrushes for painting the hall door a beautiful red. He left them in the shed and told Emma not to allow her brothers near the paint. Emma would have loved to paint the door with her dad, but he wouldn't allow her to. Instead, if there was any paint left over, he said, he would allow her to paint the door of the shed.

One day, Emma's two little brothers had fallen asleep on some blankets in the back garden while she was sitting on the swing. Their mum came out carrying an apple pie she had baked that morning. She told Emma she was going to pop next door, and she would only be a minute. 'Can I come with you?' Emma asked.

Her mum said, 'No, you stay and keep an eye on the boys.'

'Okay.'

Her mum walked around the side of the house and out the gate. Emma got off the swing and walked over to her brothers to make sure they were fast asleep, then she looked over in the direction of the shed and said to herself, 'I have an idea. While my little brothers are asleep . . .'

Her guardian angel whispered in her ear, 'No, Emma,' but she took no notice as she headed towards the shed. Again her guardian angel whispered in her ear as Emma opened the shed door, glancing back at her little brothers to make sure they were still sleeping. She walked into the shed and straight over to the can of paint. Her guardian angel kept whispering in her ear, 'No, Emma, your daddy said you were not to let your little brothers at the tin of paint.'

She spoke back to her guardian angel out loud, knowing there was no one around and that her two little brothers were asleep: 'I will not let my little brothers at the tin of paint. I only want to paint the shed door. There is nothing wrong with that.'

Emma's guardian angel whispered back to her, 'Yes, there is. Your dad said you must wait until he's painted the hall door. He's planning to start painting it when he gets home from work.'

'Go away,' said Emma to her guardian angel, 'I don't want to listen to you. You never allow me to do anything.'

Her guardian angel whispered back in her ear, 'I just don't want you to get into trouble. You are a good girl, most of the time, and I love you.'

Emma started to root around in the shed. She found a screwdriver and started to lift the lid off the tin of paint and began to stir it. She carried the tin with both hands and walked out the shed door. She put it down on the ground, before running back in to get the paintbrushes. She tore open the package they were in, and then dipped one of the brushes into the paint and started to paint the shed door, dripping paint all over the ground and on her shoes.

Emma's guardian angel whispered in her ear, 'You will get into trouble.'

She whispered back, 'I won't,' as she continued to paint the door.

*Emma painting the shed door with her guardian
angel whispering in her ear to stop.*

About ten minutes later, Emma noticed all the wet paint on the ground and on her shoes. She dropped the paintbrush and ran into the house. She looked around the kitchen for something to wipe her shoes with but, seeing nothing suitable, she decided to run up to the bathroom.

There she found a facecloth. She turned the tap on, wet the facecloth, and proceeded to wring it out.

Then she started to scrub her shoes, but the paint wasn't coming off. She said to her guardian angel, in her mind, 'I should have listened to you.'

'I love you,' her guardian angel replied. 'You better get back downstairs.'

Emma ran down the stairs and out the back door into the garden. To her horror, her two little brothers had woken up, and they were painting the shed door. Everything was a mess.

Emma screamed at them and they started to cry. She told them they were very bold, but Emma's guardian angel said to her, 'Emma, they are not bold. It is you who has been bold.'

Again, Emma told her guardian angel to go away, but her guardian angel said, 'I can never go away. I'm always here with you, Emma, and I love you.'

She carried the tin of paint back into the shed, but then she dropped the paintbrush on the ground when she heard her mum coming in the gate. As Emma's two little brothers ran towards their mum, their mum let out a scream. Johnny and Paul's hands were covered in red paint; so were their trousers and T-shirts because they had tried to wipe the paint off their hands onto their clothes.

'What has happened to Johnny and Paul?' Emma's mum asked when Emma appeared from the side of the house.

Her mum looked at her with a very cross expression, so she replied, 'It wasn't me. I only went into the bathroom for a little while and when I came out, I found the two boys had opened the tin of paint and were painting the shed door. Mum, it wasn't my fault!'

Emma's mum was very cross. She said, 'You are a brat; go to your room and take that smirk off your face.'

Emma just shrugged her shoulders. She thought it was funny seeing her two little brothers covered in paint and saying, 'It wasn't our fault.'

Emma ran up the stairs and into her room thinking, 'I can't be blamed for what my two little brothers did. It wasn't my fault. I'm not the brat – they are.'

Emma's guardian angel whispered in her ear, 'It *was* your fault, Emma – not theirs.' A few minutes later, Emma's mum called her down to help set the table for dinner. Her mum didn't say anything to her about earlier, but when her dad came home from work and dinner was over, her mum said, 'Emma, you better take your dad out to the shed.'

Johnny and Paul followed Emma and their dad outside. When their dad saw the red paint on the door and some on the ground, he asked, 'What happened?'

The two little boys, Johnny and Paul, ran up to their dad and said, 'We painted the door, Daddy!'

Emma's dad didn't say a word but turned and looked at her, before walking over to the shed. He opened the shed door and went in. He took a look around and saw the tin of paint on the cabinet and the paintbrush thrown on the ground. He turned around and said to Johnny and Paul, 'You two, go back into the house now.'

Johnny and Paul said, 'Can we not help you paint the door, Daddy?', pointing to the shed door. He said, 'No, go back into the house to your mum. I'll be in in a few minutes.'

Emma turned around to follow them, but her dad said, 'Not you, Emma. Why are you being a brat? Why are you all the time doing bold things, and then trying to blame your brothers? They are only three years of age, and no way could they have taken the tin of paint down off the cabinet, never mind find a screwdriver and open it. Look at your shoes. They are destroyed with red paint.'

Emma started to cry. She said to her dad, 'I'm sorry, Daddy, I really am.'

'Emma, what am I going to do with you? You know your mum and I love you very much and so do your brothers, but you do bold things, and sometimes, you think they are funny. Did you think what you did was funny?' asked her dad.

'Yes, I suppose I did, Dad,' she said. 'I just thought it would be great fun to paint the shed door. I knew I shouldn't have. My guardian angel told me not to.'

'Really?' asked her dad.

Emma said, 'You and Mum have always told me about my guardian angel, but I'm not very good at listening to her, Daddy.'

Her dad replied, 'So, you don't even listen to your guardian angel?'

Emma said, 'No, most of the time I ignore my guardian angel.'

'We need you to start listening to your guardian angel,' he said. 'When you know inside of you that you are not to do something, don't do it, that is your guardian angel telling you that it is wrong or bold, that you are being a brat. And for being so bold, Emma, you can clean up the shed.'

Emma protested saying, 'But Dad, the shed is in a mess.'
Emma's dad agreed with her: 'It is a mess, but it's
your job now to clean it up, and I want it spotless. When
you're finished, come into the house and
apologise to your mum. Tell her you're
sorry for being bold and for blaming
your little brothers.' He walked over to
her, put his arms around her and said,
'You know I love you, Emma. You're
my big girl, but please try and be good.'
Her dad walked out of the shed. Emma could hear
his footsteps as he walked around the side of the house.

She was standing there all alone in the shed, but not
really alone, because her guardian angel was there with
her. She started to sob a little and her guardian angel
whispered in her ear, 'It's okay, Emma.'

She spoke to her guardian angel in her mind, as she
swept the floor: 'I am going to do my best to be good
from now on. I will listen to you, my guardian angel. In
fact, I always just call you "Guardian Angel". Do you
have another name?'

Her guardian angel said, 'You don't have to change
my name – only if you wish to.'

'No,' said Emma, 'I think Guardian Angel is a beautiful name.'

Her guardian angel whispered back, 'And so is Emma.'

'Thank you,' said Emma.

When she had finished cleaning the shed, she said to her guardian angel, 'Do you think it is clean enough?'

'Yes, your dad will be very pleased. You have done a great job.'

'Thank you,' she said out loud as she closed the shed door.

She walked around the side of the house, through the back door and the kitchen, into the front room. Her mum was there, and her two little brothers were getting ready for bed. Emma said to her mum, 'I'm sorry. I'm going to try and be good from now on. I'm going to do my best.'

Her mum gave Emma a big hug and so did her two little brothers. Then Emma heard her dad coming down the stairs. When he walked into the front room, she told him she had apologised to her mum and was going to try to be good from now on.

'I'm proud of you, Emma,' he said, giving her a hug. 'Now, bedtime for my two little soldiers,' he said, picking up her brothers and carrying them upstairs to bed.

When he came back down later, he didn't say a word. Emma watched him as he went out to the shed. Looking out the kitchen window, she saw him open the shed door and disappear out of her sight for a few minutes. He emerged with the wheelbarrow, the tin of paint and the paintbrushes, plus a whole load of other stuff, and wheeled them around to the front of the house.

Emma ran into the front room to look out the window there. She saw her dad had started to clean down the hall door. Emma's guardian angel whispered in her ear, 'Go out to your dad and ask if he needs any help.'

'I don't think my dad will want my help.'

Emma's guardian angel whispered in her ear again, 'Give it a try.'

'Okay,' said Emma and went out the back door. When she got around to the front of the house, she said to her dad, 'Can I help you?'

'Of course you can, Emma,' her dad replied. 'You could get the dustpan and brush from the kitchen.'

Emma ran and got the dustpan and brush for her dad. She stood, looking up at him, and asked, 'What are you doing? What is that in your hand?'

He said to her, 'This is sandpaper. It's very rough. Touch it with your fingers.'

Emma reached out and touched it and said, 'It really is very rough. It's like little bits of glass.'

Her dad said, 'Yes, it has to be rough for the job it's going to do. Let me explain: no matter what you paint,

135

whether it's a door or a chair, or even the walls of your bedroom, everything has to be cleaned down first, so sandpaper is good for that. You rub as hard as you can in a circle like this.'

Emma watched her dad as he started to work. He continued to explain: 'Take off any dirt or loose paint, and it will make the door clean – ready for painting. There's a lot of work that you have to do first.'

Emma said, 'Can I do some of that? To help you, Dad.'

But her dad said, 'No, because it's very dusty and it would get into your eyes. It is best that I do it. That's why I'll need the dustpan and brush in a few minutes. I will call you and then you can use the dustpan and brush to take up all the powdery dust that will have fallen from the door. Inside you go now, Emma.'

She ran back into the house.

It was about half an hour later when Emma heard her dad calling her. When she went out she couldn't believe it. The doorstep was covered in a pile of dust. It was everywhere, even all over her dad's clothes. Emma touched it with her hands, and she said to her dad, 'It's like sand, but much softer.'

Her dad said, 'Yes, that's what sandpaper does, that's the way it cleans down wood. Go into the shed, Emma, and get me a bucket so we can sweep this up and put it in the bin.'

When she came back out with the bucket, her dad already had the dustpan full of some of the powdery dust and he said to Emma, 'Hold the bucket up and close your eyes, Emma.'

Emma did as her dad said, and when she opened her eyes, she saw dust all over her hands. She laughed, saying to her dad, 'My hands are white with all this dust.'

Every time her dad emptied the dustpan into the bucket, Emma closed her eyes.It took them a little while to clean it all up. Then, the two of them stood back from the hall door, admiring how it looked. It was spot-less. Emma's dad said to her, 'Put your hand on the door and feel how smooth it is.'

Emma did as her dad said, but only touched it with her fingertips because her hands were all covered in dust. 'Are we going to paint the door now?' she asked.

Her dad said, 'Not tonight because it's getting late.'

Emma felt a little disappointed but helped her dad bring everything back around to the shed in their wheel-barrow. Her dad locked the shed door this time and he gave Emma a smile. She smiled back at her dad. She knew he was making sure she didn't go into the shed again when he was at work.

As they walked back into the kitchen, her dad thanked her for helping him and for doing such a good job cleaning the shed.

He said, 'Hopefully, tomorrow after work, I will be able to paint the hall door – at least give it the first coat.'

The next day, Emma couldn't wait for her dad to get home from work. She was all excited about watching him paint the hall door, using that beautiful red paint.

When he got home, he said to her, 'I hope you are going to help me after dinner?'

Emma said, 'Yes.'

When dinner was over, Emma helped her mum clean up the kitchen while her dad got her two little brothers ready for bed.

Once her two little brothers were asleep, Emma and her dad went out the back door. She followed him around to the shed. He unlocked it and filled their wheelbarrow with all the things they needed for painting the hall door.

When they were at the front of the house, he said, 'You can put the tin of paint on the step there, Emma, and the paintbrush. I have to go back around to the shed and get a ladder.'

She did as her dad said and a minute later, he was back. He opened the can of paint and handed her the old screwdriver. He told her she could stir the paint, but she was to make sure she stirred it well.

As she started to stir, the paint seemed to get redder and redder. Emma said to her guardian angel, 'The paint is a beautiful red and I'm so glad I can help my dad.'

A few minutes later, her dad started to paint the door and Emma watched.

Every now and then, he sent her in for a glass of water. He explained that it was thirsty work.

Emma watched her dad carefully, the way he used the paintbrush, the way he made sure there wasn't too much paint on it before he brushed the door with it.

She said, 'You are very gentle painting the door with the paintbrush.'

'You have to be gentle and you have to make sure the strokes are smooth, so there is no paint running down the door. If there is paint left over, Emma, you can practise with me painting the shed door.'

When the first coat of paint had been put on the door, it looked fabulous.

The next day, Emma's dad had a day off work, so he was able to give the hall door a second coat of paint. The door looked great when it was finished.

Emma said to him, 'Our front door makes the house look brand new.'

As the two of them stood back and admired it, her dad said, 'You're right, Emma.'

She helped her dad clean up and put everything back into the wheelbarrow.

As they walked back around to the shed, her dad said, 'There is a little bit of paint left over in the tin. Do you want to paint the shed door? There is just enough paint for one coat.'

Emma said, 'I would love to, but do we have to sand it down too?'

'No, it's only an old door and not in very good condition. There's no point. We'll just give a quick clean with the sweeping brush.'

Emma told her dad that she would run in and get the sweeping brush, and off she went.

A few seconds later, she was handing the brush to her dad. He gave the door a sweep, moving the brush up and down, and back and forth.

Emma started to laugh at her dad. She thought it looked funny.

He looked at her, smiling, and said, 'This is the only way to take off the dirt!'

Emma had the paintbrush in her hand. Her guardian

angel whispered in her ear, 'Ask your dad if he could show you how to use the paintbrush again.'

Emma whispered back to her guardian angel: 'I hear you. I am listening.'

The next moment, she said to her dad, 'Can you show me how to do the first stroke? I was watching you when you were painting the hall door, but now I feel a little nervous.'

He smiled at her as she handed the paintbrush to him. He dipped the paintbrush into the tin of paint and showed Emma exactly how to do it.

He started to paint the shed door and then he handed the paintbrush back to her and said, 'You can do it.'

She dipped the brush into the tin and started to brush it gently on the door, just as her dad had.

Her dad went into the shed to look for another paintbrush. He said to Emma, 'I better paint the top of the door because you will never be able to reach it.'

'Thanks, Dad,' she said. 'I was wondering how I was going to manage to paint that part of the door.'

'This old paintbrush will do the job,' he said.

An hour later, they were finished. Emma stood back from the shed door with her dad and admired it. She said to her dad, 'Your job on the front door definitely looks better than mine.'

He said, 'For a beginner painter, it's not bad at all. In fact, I would say, Emma, it's very good.'

When Emma was in bed that night, she thanked her guardian angel. She asked her guardian angel to keep on pestering her, especially when she was ignoring what her guardian angel was saying.

Emma's guardian angel whispered back into her ear that night, just before she fell asleep: 'You are getting very good at listening. Now sleep.' And Emma closed her eyes.

CHAPTER 3

MS JULIA'S DANCE CLASS

A few weeks later in school, Emma's teacher, Ms Julia, gave them all a note to take home to their parents. Ms Julia told them the note was about a dancing class.

She also told the children that she had been a dancing teacher before she started working at their school, and she was going to start up a dance class on Fridays after school hours.

All the children in the class started to ask what kind of dancing she would teach them. Ms Julia replied, 'Irish dancing and modern dance. You can mix both and we will have lots of fun, but the lessons will cost one euro every Friday.'

Some of the children asked if the dancing would just be for their class.

Ms Julia said, 'No, it's for all of the classes.'

One of the girls, Moreen, said, 'But I have a sister in another class, so would she have to bring a euro in as well?'

'One euro is all. It is all explained in the letter,' said Ms Julia.

All the children were very excited. There was great chitchat in the classroom, and when the bell rang, they all said goodbye to their teacher and began to leave.

As soon as Emma arrived home, she showed the note to her mum. She told her mum everything Ms Julia had said.

'Can I do the dance class, Mum?' she asked.

Emma's mum replied that she wasn't sure. 'I know it's only one euro every week, Emma, but you know your dad doesn't earn much money at the moment. We will see what we can do.' Then she added, 'Would you go outside and take the washing off the line for me, Emma?'

Emma said, 'Yes.' She picked up the basket and walked out to the clothesline. She spoke to her guardian angel in her mind and asked what she could do to help her mum and dad more.

Emma's guardian angel whispered back into her ear, 'There is no more you can do.'

'But there must be something I can do,' said Emma, 'What if Dad and Mum can't afford that one euro?'

The basket was now full of washing, so Emma went to pick it up.

She spoke again to her guardian angel as she walked slowly back to the house: 'Maybe I could help my neighbours doing some little jobs like I do for my mum, and maybe I could make up one euro a week. Dolly next door is on her own. Her son is away most of the time. I could help her with some things?'

Emma's guardian angel whispered in her ear, 'You will have to get permission from your mum and dad.'

'Okay,' said Emma as she walked slowly, taking little steps towards the back door.

Just before she reached the back door, she said to her guardian angel, 'I could do the garden. I could wash and dry dishes. I could hang washing on the line. I could even go down to the shops. I could just sweep and polish the floor. I could do loads of things, just like I do for my mum. I could also do some jobs like that for Dolly. Maybe some of our other neighbours would like me to do some jobs too.'

Emma's guardian angel whispered back into her ear, 'First of all, don't forget, you must ask for permission from your mum and dad, Emma.'

At the same time as her guardian angel spoke to her, Emma reached up and opened the back door. She walked into the kitchen with the washing and then she folded it up, before carrying it upstairs and putting it away.

She couldn't wait for her dad to get home from work that day. When her mum asked her to set the table for dinner, she was excited because she knew her dad would be home soon.

Her mum said, 'Get your two little brothers, Emma. Get them to sit at the table.'

Emma went into the front room. Her two little brothers were playing with cars on the floor. She said, 'Dinner's ready.'

The two of them went into the kitchen with her and sat up at the table.

Then Emma heard the key turning in the front door. It was her dad. He was home from work. He came into the kitchen and said, 'That food smells great,' and gave her mum a big hug. 'I am so hungry,' he said, 'I could eat an elephant.'

Then he went over to Emma and her two little brothers and kissed each of them on the forehead. He said, 'I hope you were all good today for your mum.'

The three of them said, 'Yes we were, Daddy.'

Their dad went to the kitchen sink and washed his hands, to help their mum serve up dinner.

Just as they were finishing their food, Emma said, 'I got a letter from my teacher today about dancing after school on Fridays, Daddy, and it will only cost one euro. Please, say I can do dancing?'

Emma's dad looked at her mum, who said, 'Emma would love to do the dancing. She's been so excited about the idea of learning how to dance.'

Her dad looked across the table at her and saw a pleading look on his daughter's face. He said to her, 'Emma, we will put a euro away every week for you, but there might be occasions when you will have to miss a dance class.'

It was at that moment that Emma's guardian angel whispered in her ear and said, 'Now is the time for you to tell them your idea.'

Emma did exactly as her guardian angel said. 'Dad, I could do some jobs for Dolly next door. She might be able to give me a few cents, and maybe I could do some jobs for old Mr Murphy too. I could take his dog out for a walk and maybe he would give me a few cents too. He's always been asking if someone would take his dog for a walk, even once a week.'

Her mum said, 'Let's think about that,' and her dad nodded.

He said, 'First, I would have to go and talk to the neighbours and make sure that would be okay. Maybe we should just ask Dolly first.'

Emma jumped up straight away and said, 'Dad, come next door to Dolly's right now, and let's ask her.'

Emma's dad was a little bit hesitant but gave in.

The two of them went next door. Dolly was delighted to see them and welcomed them into her home, where she offered them a cup of tea.

Emma's dad said, 'No, thank you. We have just finished dinner.'

Emma said, 'My dad wants to ask you whether, if I did a few jobs for you every week, you could afford to give me a few cents. It will be towards my dance class.'

'Dance class?' said Dolly.

'Yes,' said Emma. 'Our new teacher, Ms Julia, is actually a dancing teacher as well and she's going to hold a class on Fridays after school for everyone. It will be a euro every Friday.'

Dolly thought for a minute and then she said, 'There are loads of jobs that need doing here in the house that I can't do on my own. If you, Emma, could give me a helping hand, it would definitely be worth it. I will give you ten cents for every job you do for me.'

Emma was delighted. She looked at her dad and said, 'Can I? Can I?'

He said, 'Yes, but you must always tell your mum when you're going into Dolly's to do a job, so your mum won't be looking for you.'

'Okay,' Emma said, and just as they were going out of Dolly's hall door, she asked Dolly, 'Could I start tomorrow? I'll come in after school, as soon as I'm finished doing the jobs for my mum.'

'Yes, that would be great,' Dolly replied. 'Looking forward to seeing you tomorrow, Emma.'

Emma ran back into the house to tell her mum, leaving her dad and Dolly talking.

As they walked down the path to the gate, Dolly said to Emma's dad, 'It's not about the jobs. It will be the company of Emma coming to visit me every day or as many days as she can that makes a difference to me.'

Dolly thanked Emma's dad and they said goodbye.

When he came back into the front room, Emma said, 'Thank you!' and gave him a big hug.

'You are welcome. Now, it's time for bed.'

When Friday came and school was over, there were thirty-eight children of all ages ready to start the first dance class. The children helped take the desks and chairs out of the biggest classroom and put them into the other two smaller classrooms. They had the job done in no time at all and the floor was swept too.

Ms Julia said, 'This will have to be done every Friday before we start, and at the end of dance class, we have to put the desks back into this room.'

Then she had all the children line up and she took down all their names and ages.

Ten minutes later, she said, 'Let's all get ready now for our first dance lesson.'

Ms Julia put the children into different groups according to their age. The younger ones lined up at the front and the older, taller children lined up at the back. She moved them in staggered rows of eight so she could walk between them, showing them how to move their feet and hands and how to move their whole body.

The children loved it. The hour passed so quickly.

Then there was a quick tidy-up of all the desks. All the children told Ms Julia that they were looking forward to next Friday.

Ms Julia asked to them to practise their steps with each other during the week, even in the playground.

They all said goodbye and headed home.

When Emma arrived home, she showed her mum and dad and her two little brothers, Johnny and Paul, the few steps she had learned. Her mum was surprised that she had learned so much and so quickly.

Emma said, 'I wonder, is there any dancing on the TV? Could you turn it on?'

Her mum looked through the channels but found nothing that would help with dancing.

Then her mum reminded Emma to go into Dolly next door and do whatever little job that Dolly wanted her to do, and to come straight back home afterwards.

'Okay,' said Emma, and she ran to Dolly's house.

She knocked on the door and Dolly opened it. Dolly was delighted to see her. When she asked Emma about her dance class, Emma told her everything and even showed her the few steps she had learned.

Emma helped Dolly tidy the kitchen, and when Emma was leaving, she asked, 'What would you like me to do tomorrow?'

Dolly replied, 'Tomorrow is Saturday, Emma. I wasn't expecting you to do a job over the weekend.'

Emma hesitated and then said, 'Maybe not every Saturday, now that I think of it, but any Saturday I can, I will. And of course, during the week, I'll come over as many days as my mum allows me to.'

'That would be perfect,' said Dolly. 'If the day is fine tomorrow, it would be great if you could sweep the path all around the garden, and if there are any papers, pick them up. Of course, I will give you a hand as well and you can tell me all about what has happened in school during the week.'

'Okay,' said Emma. 'Goodbye.'

'See you tomorrow,' said Dolly.

The next morning, when Emma went to Dolly's to sweep the garden path, Dolly had a surprise for her.

When Emma knocked on the front door, Dolly opened it and said, 'I have something on the table for you.'

Emma saw a beautiful box on the table. It was a tin box, but it was unusual. It was shaped like a little house.

Dolly said to Emma, 'It's a savings box, and there is already some money in it towards your dance lessons.'

Emma went over, picked the box up and gave it a shake. She could hear all the coins rattling inside. She put it back down on the table and said thank you to Dolly, and gave her a hug. 'I can't wait to show it to my two brothers and my mum and dad,' she said, 'but you said you want me to sweep the path and do some tidying up around the house, so I'll do that first.'

Dolly said, 'Follow me.'

They went into a little room next to the kitchen. Dolly handed Emma a big brush and picked up the dustpan and brush for herself. Dolly also took a plastic bag out of the cabinet.

The two of them went out into the garden, and in no time at all, the sweeping and tidying up was done. Dolly was very happy with all the work that Emma had helped her to do.

Emma said goodbye to Dolly as she went out the door, holding on to her new savings box.

She carried it into her house and put it on the kitchen table. She didn't say a word to her mum or her brothers. She just wanted it to be a surprise for them to see it there on the table.

She got herself a glass of water and sat up at the table, waiting for her mum and two little brothers to come in. She could hear them upstairs, and when they came down and opened the door, her mum said, 'Emma, what's that on the table?'

Emma replied cheerfully, 'Dolly gave me a savings box and there is already some money in it towards my dancing!'

Emma's two little brothers were very excited, and they climbed up on the chairs at the table to touch the savings box.

Admiring it, Emma's mum opened the box and, together, they counted the money that was in it. All the loose change added up to one euro.

Emma's mum said, 'That one euro will do for what-ever week your dad does not have a euro for your dancing.'

Emma said to her mum, 'Dolly is very kind.'

Chapter 4

The Dance Show

The weeks passed. Emma was enjoying school. More and more children joined the dance class and soon all the children in the school were taking the dance lessons.

One day, Ms Julia announced to the class, 'Before school ends for the summer, we're going to put on a little dance show. We would love all your parents to come.'

The children were very excited about the show. Ms Julia decided to have another class during the week: dancing wasn't just on a Friday anymore but on Wednesdays as well.

She handed out another letter for all the children to take home. In this letter, Ms Julia explained to the class and their parents that she wanted every child, the boys and girls, to ask their mums and dads if it would it be possible for them to make a costume for the show.

'Maybe your mum has an old dress or maybe your dad has an old jacket that could be made smaller,' Ms Julia suggested.

As soon as Emma got home from school, she handed

her mum the letter and even before her mum opened it, Emma asked her, 'Could you make a costume for me? Maybe out of one of your dresses? Maybe from a dress you don't want anymore?'

Emma's mum looked at her as she opened the letter and she gave Emma a big smile. She said, 'After dinner, you can come upstairs with me and we will have a look in my wardrobe. Now set the table for dinner and get your brothers in. Your dad will be home any minute.'

Emma did as her mum asked, and then she heard her dad turning the key in the door. Her dad walked straight into the kitchen and gave her mum a hug and a kiss as he always did.

Then, he turned to the twins and to Emma and said, 'I hope you were good for your mum today.'

Emma said, 'Yes we were, Dad.'

She couldn't wait to be sitting at the dinner table.

As soon as they sat down, she said to her dad, 'Mum is going to make a costume for me. We are putting a dance show on in school, just before the holidays.'

Emma's dad looked at her mum. Her mum nodded and said, 'Yes, that's right. When dinner is over, Emma and I are going to go up and have a look in the wardrobe to see what we can find.'

Emma sat at the table with her two little brothers while her mum and dad served up dinner.

When dinner was over, the table was cleared. Emma's dad was washing the dishes. Emma walked over to the door to take down a dishcloth, but her dad said, 'No, Emma, you and your mum go upstairs and have a good look in that wardrobe. Off you go now, and I will mind Johnny and Paul.'

Johnny and Paul were playing on the floor in the kitchen, rolling a ball to each other.

Emma ran upstairs and into her mum's bedroom, followed by her mum. They took almost all of her mum's dresses out of the wardrobe while deciding which one they could use to make a costume.

Her mum held up a beautiful blue dress and said to Emma, 'I haven't worn this dress for years now. The last time I wore it, you were only a year old. I think it's okay for me to turn it into a beautiful dress for you, Emma.'

Her mum went over to one of the bedside lockers, opened the top drawer and took out some bright-coloured ribbon. One ribbon was yellow and the other was red.

She said, 'I think this will do. We can put a bow at the collar and do the same for the waistline.'

Emma was so excited. She gave her mum a big hug and said, 'Thank you, Mum, so much.'

Everything else was put back into the wardrobe as neat and tidy as it was before.

The two of them went downstairs when they were finished. Emma's mum carried down the blue dress and Emma carried down the red and yellow ribbons to show them to her dad, and Johnny and Paul.

Emma's mum said, 'I think you children should go to bed now and tomorrow, Emma, I will start making your costume while you are at school.'

The next morning, Emma went off to school and she told her teacher, Ms Julia, that her mum was going to make her a costume from her beautiful blue dress.

Months passed quickly and in no time at all, it was time to put on the dance show. Ms Julia and Principal Martha went to see the parish priest to get permission to use the parish hall because the school did not have a large enough space. The priest said to Ms Julia, 'You will have to get some volunteers to clean up the hall. It is in a bit of a mess and it's quite dusty.'

Ms Julia replied, 'No problem at all.'

Again Ms Julia gave a letter to all the children. This

time it asked if the parents would volunteer to clean up the parish hall and decorate it before the show. If they could help, they were to turn up on Saturday, about twelve o'clock.

On Saturday, Emma and her dad went down to the parish hall. They took a sweeping brush, a bucket and some cloths with them. When they arrived, there was a large crowd of parents there already. They were all very busy.

Emma spoke to her guardian angel and said, 'This is great. Everyone is helping to get the hall ready for our dance show. Everyone must have listened to their own guardian angels.'

Emma's guardian angel said, 'You're right, Emma, they did.'

By four o'clock, the parish hall was spotless, so Emma and her dad headed home.

Two weeks later, all the parents received another letter in the post. It reminded them that the concert would take place in two weeks' time, at twelve o'clock on a Saturday in the parish hall.

When the letter arrived, Emma and her mum were working on her costume. Emma said to her mum as she danced around the kitchen table, 'Only two weeks to go!' Emma was forever dancing, and sometimes, she would ask her guardian angel, 'Are you dancing with me?'

Her guardian angel would whisper back, 'Yes, I'm dancing with you, Emma.'

Soon enough it was the day before the show. At school, just as the Friday dance lesson ended, Ms Julia said to the class, 'I want you all to turn up at ten in the morning tomorrow so we can do a little practise on the stage, and don't forget to be wearing your costume.'

As some of the children were walking out of the class, one said to their teacher, 'I hope you will like my costume. My mum worked very hard at it.'

Another child said, 'My mum couldn't do my costume, but my dad did it for me.'

One little girl said, 'My granny made my costume for me.'

'Now, all go home and be good for your parents,' Ms Julia said. 'And go to bed early because we have a long day tomorrow. We have a show to put on.'

The children all left, happily.

Emma was so excited about the show. Her mum had her costume hanging on the door of the wardrobe. After dinner, she asked her to come upstairs with her to try it on. Emma thought it was so beautiful as she looked at herself in the mirror. Even her gleaming white socks looked great.

Emma went downstairs with her mum to show her costume to her dad and her two little brothers.

Her dad said to Emma, 'You look so pretty, but don't forget your shoes. You can't go in your stocking feet.'

'Where are my shoes?' Emma asked.

Her dad took them out from under the chair and said, 'Here they are.'

They were shiningly clean. Emma said thanks to her dad for cleaning her shoes so well. They looked brand new.

That night when Emma was in bed, she said her prayers and thanked God. She said to her guardian angel, 'I do hope that I don't make any mistakes dancing tomorrow or that any of the others don't make a mistake.'

Her guardian angel said, 'No, you won't make any mistakes, Emma, and neither will the other children. Now, it's time to go to sleep. Close your eyes.'

Emma's eyes started to get heavy and she fell asleep.

The next morning, she woke up at eight o'clock. Her mum and dad were already up getting breakfast ready. Her two little brothers were sitting at the kitchen table.

'I don't have enough time to get everything ready,' said Emma.

Her dad said, 'Yes you do. You still have lots of time.'

When breakfast was over, Emma's two little brothers wanted to wear their good clothes too. So, Emma helped them to get dressed and then she went upstairs with her mum to put on her costume. Her mum did her hair, and in no time at all, it was half nine; almost time to walk down to the village.

Emma spoke to her guardian angel in her mind and said, 'Thank you for keeping the rain away.'

'You're welcome,' said Emma's guardian angel.

A few minutes later, the whole family walked out the hall door and down to the little village, heading for the parish hall.

When they arrived, there were already a lot of children there with their parents, and Ms Julia had some of the children on stage practising.

Emma's mum said, 'You better go backstage now, Emma. If you need us, give us a wave from the stage.'

'Okay,' said Emma and she ran off. She rehearsed her part six times on stage, but once the time reached half eleven, no one was allowed on stage anymore. All the children were backstage, waiting anxiously for the show to start.

The principal went out onto the stage first to welcome all the parents. She thanked them for coming to watch the children put on the show.

Then Ms Julia came out and introduced the first group of girls and boys that were to dance. Their dance was called 'The Dancing Frogs'.

Ms Julia did this for every group of children.

Soon it was time for Emma's class to go on stage. Ms Julia introduced the dance, which was called 'Dancing Stones'.

Just as Emma was going out onto the stage with the other boys and girls, she spoke in her mind to her guardian angel: 'I'm so nervous and I know my friends are too. Don't let us make any mistakes.'

Emma's guardian angel whispered back into her ear, 'You will all dance like feathers, gracefully.'

When Emma was on the stage dancing with her friends, she forgot all about being nervous or afraid, and so did the other children. They just enjoyed themselves, and when they were finished, they bowed.

When all of the classes had done their dances, all the children were called out onto the stage to bow together. The parents clapped and cheered. Lots of photographs were taken and there was lots of laughter.

Afterwards Ms Julia told all the children how brilliant they were and wished them a great summer holiday. The parents said goodbye to each other and to the children.

Emma's guardian angel dancing with her on stage.

When Emma got home, her parents told her that she had been brilliant on the stage and had looked beautiful. 'All the costumes were fantastic,' said her mum, 'and I loved the way some of the boys wore caps.'

Emma gave her mum a hug and said, 'Thank you for making my costume. It was so beautiful. I know you loved that blue dress as well. It didn't look shabby or anything. I know you could have worn it again in the summer.'

Her mum replied, 'It's only a dress and it made a beautiful costume for you.'

Emma gave her mum another hug and a few minutes later, she said, 'Goodnight,' to her dad. Her little brothers were already in bed. Emma got into bed herself and she said to her guardian angel, 'Goodnight and thank you for today.'

Emma closed her eyes and fell fast asleep.

CYRIL

CHAPTER 1

CYRIL'S SCHOOL TRIP

One day, when Cyril was twelve years old, he went on a school tour. He was sitting by a window in the bus, daydreaming, as the bus headed up into the Wicklow mountains. It was having difficulty climbing uphill. It slowed down and almost came to a stop. The bus driver asked for everyone to sit down in their seats. Cyril could hear the engine screeching as the bus started to struggle up the hill again. Suddenly the bus driver, Paul, shouted, 'We made it!' and all the children gave the bus driver a cheer and clapped their hands.

A few miles further up the road, the bus slowed down again but this time, it wasn't struggling to climb a hill. The driver had slowed down to pull out into the middle of the road. As Cyril continued gazing out the window he saw the bus was overtaking young men in T-shirts, shorts and trainers. They were running on the mountain roads. Cyril never took his eyes off them.

His guardian angel whispered in his ear, 'Cyril, you would be good at that sport.'

Cyril replied in his mind and said, 'But I am no good at any sport. How on earth would I be good at running?'

Cyril's guardian angel whispered in his ear again: 'You won't know unless you try.'

Within a minute or two, they had passed the runners on the road. Cyril continued looking out the window, daydreaming; imagining those young men still running alongside the bus.

The bus slowed down yet again and pulled out. They drove slowly past a young man running uphill by himself. Cyril watched the man's arms going back and forth, bent at the elbow each time one of his feet touched the ground. Cyril noticed the muscles in his legs. He stood up in his seat and put his nose against the window of the bus so he could keep on watching the young man running uphill.

'I think you're wrong,' Cyril said to his guardian angel, 'because I don't have muscles like that runner. Everyone calls me scrawny.'

His guardian angel whispered back to him, 'Your body will change as you grow. It won't always be scrawny. Think about it. So maybe when you get into secondary, you will have grown that little bit more. You might be surprised by how much taller you will have gotten and

Cyril looking out the school bus window in
amazement at the man running on the country road.

stronger, by the time you start secondary school after
the summer holidays.'

Cyril gave a sigh and sat back down in his seat. He
daydreamed a little more, wondering if his guardian
angel was right. He imagined himself running beside the
runner he had just seen.

A short while later, the bus reached its destination
and all his schoolmates had a great day up in the
Wicklow mountains. They especially enjoyed the

waterfall flowing down the mountain and into the lake, and having fun along the shores of the lake, where they sat on rocks or on tufts of grass and ate their sandwiches.

Afterwards, they sent flat stones skidding over the surface of the water to see whose stone would hop the furthest. Then they walked along the many paths and among the trees. It was a lot of walking but it was great fun. They walked through the ancient graveyard next to the old church, and everyone stopped to admire the enormous Celtic cross in the middle of the graveyard.

A few hours later, the teachers told all the students to head back to the bus. It was a long walk but all of the boys from Cyril's class had great fun.

The bus driver, Paul, let out a shout: 'Hurry up there, lads, and get on the bus. We are running a bit late. We don't want your parents to be worried.'

Everybody had gotten onto the bus and was sitting in their seats when their teacher Mrs Smith called out the name of every pupil to make sure nobody was left behind.

Two and a half hours later, they pulled into the schoolyard. Their parents were there waiting. Before any of the boys got off the bus, Mrs Smith said, 'If there is no one here to pick you up, walk back over to me.' But all the boys shouted that they could see their mum and some shouted they could see their dad.

When Cyril got off the bus, he could see his mum waving and hear her calling him. His mum was standing outside the gate waiting for him. Cyril said goodbye to his friends and hurried over to his mum.

Cyril said to his mum, 'I thought you would have brought the car?'

His mum replied, 'I needed the exercise. I haven't gotten out all day for a walk. It will only take us half an hour, Cyril, if we walk briskly.'

They walked home together through the town and up along some country roads. Cyril lived just on the outskirts of the town and as they were walking his mum said, 'I can't wait to hear about your day out.'

Cyril burst out laughing with excitement. 'You won't believe it, Mum. The bus was making a whole load of squeaky noises as it struggled up one of the hills on the mountain roads. I didn't think the bus was going to make it,' he said to his mum, 'I thought it was going to roll back down the hill. The driver told us all to sit in our seats. It was a little bit scary, but when we reached the top we all gave the driver a big cheers and clapped Then later on we passed a group of young men running. And when we got there, we had great fun down at the lake,

Mum, and that's where we had a picnic. The day just flew and I'm exhausted now.'

Cyril's mum said to him, 'Well, it is late – it's nearly nine o'clock. So, when you get home you can have a snack and I think you should go to bed.'

'I'm glad there's no school in the morning,' he said.

Chapter 2

Thinking about Running

On Saturday morning, Cyril's mum asked him if he could cut the grass and maybe do some weeding in the flowerbed, just at the end of the garden.

'Mum, do I have to?'

His mum said, 'Yes, I need a helping hand.'

Cyril's guardian angel whispered in his ear: 'Help your mum.'

So he said, 'Okay,' and headed over to the shed to get the lawnmower and the other gardening tools he would need, including the clippers, a rake and a little shovel to do the weeding.

Cyril's mum was standing at the back door and she called to him, 'Don't forget to put the gardening gloves on, so you don't get any blisters or a thorn in your fingers.'

'Thanks, Mum,' he shouted back, remembering the last time he was pulling weeds and cut his finger. He ran back into the shed to grab a pair of gloves.

It took a while to cut the grass, rake it into piles and then put it into a bucket and empty it out into the corner of the garden where all the debris went. While he was doing this, he spoke to his guardian angel in a low voice, knowing that no one else could hear him. 'Since I was little I have called you Swift,' he said. 'Did you give me that name?'

Cyril's guardian angel whispered back to him, 'Yes.'

Cyril was puzzled. He was just about to say something when his guardian angel said, 'Cyril, do you not remember? You were sitting on that rock there beside the flowerbed, where you are standing now. You were only three years of age. You stood up but lost your balance and at that moment, you caught a glimpse of me when I reached out and broke your fall so you did not hurt yourself. You laughed and I whispered in your ear, Swift, and from that day on, you called me Swift.'

'I don't remember falling,' said Cyril, 'but I do remember saying the word Swift when I was little.'

Swift whispered to him, 'Children usually forget but you didn't.'

Cyril continued weeding the flowerbed, speaking silently to his guardian angel. 'That rock looks small now to me, but I guess when I was three, it looked very big. I remember sitting on it.' Then Cyril stood up and looked around with a big smile on his face, before saying to Swift, 'I wish I could get a glimpse of you again.'

His guardian angel whispered back to him, 'Not this time, Cyril. One day, maybe.'

Cyril said, 'Only maybe?'

His guardian angel said, 'Yes, only maybe.'

'When my mum says maybe to me when I ask for something, it always means no,' Cyril said disappointedly.

When all the weeding was finished in the flowerbed, he put all the tools away and as he was locking the shed, he said to Swift, 'Do you really think I could be good at running?'

'You won't know unless you try,' replied his guardian angel.

When Cyril went into the kitchen, his mum said, 'You better wash those hands and especially under your nails.'

'Mum, you don't have to keep on telling me things like that. I'm twelve now. I know.'

'I'm just reminding you,' she said.

Cyril turned on the tap at the kitchen sink, washed his hands and scrubbed his nails with the nail brush as there was loads of dirt under them. Then he went over and sat at the kitchen table. He said to his mum, 'When I was a toddler, were there any particular words that I said a lot?'

His mum looked up at him and said, 'What a strange question to ask.'

'I was just wondering.'

'No,' she said, 'nothing I can remember. Cyril, would you go upstairs and bring down your school uniform?'

He got up from the table and just as he was going out the kitchen door, his mum said, 'I do remember one word you said an awful lot when you were about three years of age. You used to run around the garden saying the word "swift". We didn't know where you got that word from. We thought maybe the radio or the TV, but you definitely didn't get it from me or your dad. It's a hard word to say for a little child, but you seemed to be constantly repeating it, especially when you were out in the garden.'

Cyril said, 'Thanks, Mum,' and ran up the stairs and picked his school uniform up off the floor where he had thrown it.

On the way back downstairs, he spoke to his guardian angel, silently in his mind: 'My mum remembers me saying your name, Swift.'

His guardian angel didn't reply. When Cyril stepped off the last step of the stairs, he said, 'Thank you, my guardian angel, Swift.'

A few months later, Cyril walked into the house to find his dad watching the sports channel on the TV. He was watching athletics – the hundred-metre sprint. Cyril stood at the dining room door with his mouth open. He couldn't believe it. They were running so fast and the race was over in seconds. 'I wonder if I could ever run like that?' he thought to himself. His guardian angel whispered in his ear, 'It's not just about winning. It's about enjoying the sport.'

Cyril walked over to his dad, who was sitting on the couch, and sat down beside him. His dad looked at him and said, 'Since when are you interested in sport?'

Cyril looked up at his dad. 'Remember, Dad, me telling you about my school tour a few months ago and seeing the group of men running up the mountain? I've been interested since then.'

'Oh, I see,' said his dad. 'Did you tell your sports teacher you're interested in running?'

'No, I was always told I was no good,' he said. 'No one ever picked me for any teams. But I'm interested in the running idea, Dad.'

His dad said, 'Cyril, stand up there in front of me and let me have a look at you.' His dad got up off the couch and lifted up Cyril's arms. 'Your arms and legs are still a bit scrawny, but maybe in the summer, when school is over, I can take you down to the running club and see what the coach thinks about you building up your muscle and becoming a runner. I don't know much about running, but I think you should give it a go.'

Cyril was so excited. He said, 'Do you think I would be able to run in races?'

His dad said, 'Of course, why not? You have to give everything in life a try.'

Cyril jumped up and down with excitement. His dad said to him, 'If you don't want to watch the racing, out you go. If you do, sit quietly.'

Cyril sat back down on the couch with his dad and watched every single race. He watched every step the runners took, and watched how the winners waved to all the people in the stands. When the races were over, his dad turned to Cyril and said, 'You really must be interested. You have sat there glued to the TV watching every race.'

Cyril looked up at his dad and said, 'Yes, I am.'

Then his dad said to him, 'Being a runner will mean practising every day.'

Then the motor car racing started on the sports channel. His dad said, 'We will talk about it again when you get to your summer holidays. You can go out now.'

'Thanks, Dad.' Cyril got up and went out to meet some of his friends.

He thought school would never be over and summer would never come. He couldn't wait to start running.

One day, Cyril's guardian angel whispered in his ear,

'Ask your mum if she wants anything from the shops. You could walk down and get it instead of your mum using the car. The walking will help to build up your legs for running.'

'Do I have to?' Cyril replied in his mind. 'It is much easier going down in the car with Mum and helping her.'

Swift whispered back, 'I thought you wanted to become a runner?'

Cyril said in his mind, 'I do, but I'm still worried I won't be any good.'

'You will never know unless you try,' Swift replied. 'Don't be lazy.'

Cyril got up and said, 'Okay.' He spoke to his mum and she gave him a short shopping list, and off he went to the shop.

As the days passed, Cyril continued to help his mum by walking to the shops for her. One day, on his way there, he met some of his friends. They were all heading down to the sports field. They were carrying haversacks on their backs and they all had tracksuits on. Cyril walked with them part of the way. He said to his friend, Tommy, 'Do you think I would be good at any sport? If I joined the sports club in the summer?'

Tommy looked at his friend and said to him, 'I don't think you would be any good at football, Cyril, I think it would be too physical for you. But there are loads of other sports. There's handball, running, tennis. Maybe you would be good at one of them?'

Cyril's eyes lit up when his friend said running. He wanted to tell Tommy he was thinking of trying running, and tell him about the runners in the Wicklow mountains and the sprinters on TV. But at that moment his friend said, 'I have to go now, Cyril. See you later,' and he ran to catch up with the others.

Cyril stood there on the corner waiting for the lights to change so he could cross the road to the shops. He felt really happy. It was the first time any of his friends had given him encouragement about sport. He said thank you to his guardian angel and asked him, 'Did you have anything to do with what Tommy said?'

Cyril's guardian angel whispered in his ear: 'Yes, I spoke to Tommy's guardian angel.'

'What did you say to Tommy's guardian angel?'

'Never mind,' said Swift. 'Now, go and do the shopping for your mum.'

So Cyril went around the supermarket, getting a few bits and bobs for his mum. There were only another six weeks of school left, he thought to himself, and then it would be the summer holidays and he could join the sports club.

On his way home, as he walked with the shopping bag, he swapped it from one hand to another, trying to build up the muscles in his arms.

As soon as he got home, he put the groceries away for his mum.

Those last weeks passed quickly, and soon it was the last day of school. Everyone was so happy – the summer holidays were here and there would be no more homework. That day, Cyril walked home from school with Tommy and he told him that his dad had said he could join the sports club. Cyril asked, 'What day would be best for me to go down with my dad? I know there is always something on in the sports club every day, even the evenings.'

Tommy said, 'I don't think it will matter what day you and your dad go down to the sports club. It's open all day and in the evening time during the summer. I'm going down this evening to do some football training. Maybe your dad would bring you down tonight?'

Cyril said, 'I'll ask him. I hope he gets home from work early enough. He does work late some evenings, but that's not too often.'

The two boys went into a shop and bought some sweets. They sat on a wall by the green in town and ate them, in no hurry to get home. Cyril told Tommy for the first time how interested he was in running and how excited he was about joining the club. Tommy told Cyril all about the training he did for his football, and even showed Cyril some exercises. The two boys practised them on the green.

Every now and then, Cyril burst out laughing and said, 'I'm not very good at these exercises,' but Tommy gave him loads of encouragement, telling him, 'It takes practice. I wasn't very good at them either when I started, but I love it now.'

After that, the two boys continued on their journey home. As they reached Tommy's housing estate, the two boys said goodbye, and five minutes later Cyril was home.

CHAPTER 3

JOINING THE SPORTS CLUB

When Cyril got home his mum wasn't there. There was no car in the driveway, so he guessed she was down at the shops.

A few minutes later, he heard the car pulling into the drive. When his mum came into the kitchen, she said to him, 'It's your summer holidays. What have you got planned, Cyril?'

His mum was expecting him to say 'nothing in particular', but it was a great surprise when Cyril said, 'I'm going to join the sports club. I'm just waiting on Dad to come home.'

'Good for you!' said his mum. She was very happy to hear this.

'My friend, Tommy, is in the football club in the sports centre. I'm going to join the running club. When will Dad be home? I hope he's not working late, Mum.'

Cyril's mum said, 'No, he isn't. He'll be home around six.'

As soon as Cyril's dad got home from work, Cyril said to him, 'I hope you haven't forgotten, Dad. You said you'd let me join the running club. Can we go tonight?'

'It's the school holidays already?' said his dad.

'Yes,' Cyril said as he stood in the kitchen, waiting for his dad to say they would go tonight after dinner, but that didn't happen.

'I'm too tired now,' his dad replied. 'I had a hard day in work. But we will head down in the morning as it's a Saturday.'

Cyril was a little disappointed, but said, 'Thanks, Dad.'

He knew his dad worked very hard, but when he went to bed that night, he had loads of dreams of running across the mountains. The next morning, Swift whispered again and again in Cyril's ear to wake up. Cyril opened his eyes eventually, after twisting and turning many times, saying 'Leave me alone' to his guardian angel.

Swift whispered into his ear, 'Your dad is already downstairs having breakfast, waiting on you.'

Cyril opened his eyes and sat up in bed. He looked across the room at the clock on the cabinet – it read ten o'clock. He was shocked. He had slept in so late. He said to his guardian angel, 'I was dreaming of racing across the mountains.'

Swift whispered in his ear, 'You better get dressed and get down and have breakfast.'

Cyril dressed quickly. He ran down the stairs and in through the kitchen door. His dad said, 'Good morning, sleepyhead. Cyril, I thought you wanted to go down to the sports club?'

'Yes, I do,' he said as he sat down at the breakfast table.

'You better have a real hearty breakfast,' said his dad as his mum gave him a bowl of porridge, a boiled egg and a slice of toast cut into fingers for dipping into his egg.

Twenty minutes later, his dad said, 'Are you ready to go?'

Cyril said, 'Yes, I just want to go upstairs. I'll be back down in a minute.'

'Hurry up,' his dad said.

As Cyril legged it up the stairs, he said to Swift, 'I'm feeling a little nervous.' Then as he went into the bathroom to brush his teeth, his guardian angel whispered in his ear, 'There is no need to be nervous. You are just overexcited. Take a deep breath.'

He took a deep breath as he looked into the mirror over the sink. 'All done,' he said out loud to himself, and then he went back down the stairs and into the kitchen.

'Let's go,' he said to his dad as he grabbed his jacket and went out the back door.

His dad called after him, 'Hold on a minute. I have to get my jacket.'

Cyril stood at the back door and shouted, 'Hurry up!'

A minute later, he was walking down to the sports club with his dad.

As they approached the sports club grounds, he saw some of his friends out on the pitch doing exercises and some other boys and girls running around the track. They walked through the gate and into the clubhouse. They stood there for a minute, looking around, and then his dad went up to one of the men that was standing in one of the corridors, shouting at some boys and girls to hurry up and get out onto the pitch. He introduced himself and Cyril and asked, 'Would it be possible to talk with one of the coaches here?'

The man asked his dad what sport Cyril was interested in. Cyril spoke up straight away and said, 'Running.'

'I'm Coach Mark and I'm one of the coaches at the athletics club,' the man said. 'Give me a few minutes so I can give these boys and girls some work to do.' Mark went out one of the doors with the boys and girls, and Cyril and his dad waited in the corridor.

Cyril's dad said to him, 'That's good, we met the right coach straight away. Don't be nervous, Cyril.'

'I'm not nervous now. I'm just so excited.'

The next minute, the door opened and Coach Mark walked over to them, asking, 'Cyril, have you done any athletics before?'

'No, I've done no sport at all.'

Mark then looked at him with a kind of curiosity on his face and asked, 'Why have you all of a sudden decided now?'

So Cyril told Mark the story about seeing the young men running in the mountains and how that was the day he decided he would love to be a runner.

Mark said to Cyril, 'Do you think you could win any medals?'

Cyril said, 'I will try. I will give it all my best and I know I will enjoy it.'

Mark said, 'Follow me.'

Cyril and his dad followed the coach into a room where Cyril had his height and weight measured. Mark said, 'You have long legs and that's good for running. Did you bring a tracksuit with you?'

'Yes.'

The coach said to Cyril's dad, 'There is a form you will need to fill out for your son,' and handed him a clipboard with papers and a pen attached. Cyril's dad sat down and started to fill it out. Mark said, 'Cyril can start now. But seeing as you have done no running or no sport, Cyril, before we get you running, we're going to have to build your body up slowly. We don't want you to get hurt in any way. There's the changing room on your left – go and get changed and we'll get started.'

Cyril went in and changed into his tracksuit and trainers. When he came out, Mark was talking to his dad. He turned and looked at Cyril. He said, 'The tracksuit is fine,' but then he turned to Cyril's dad and said, 'You will have to get your son better trainers than those.' He wrote down on a piece of paper the type of trainers Cyril would need, and also told his dad he would need some shorts and T-shirts.

Mark and Cyril's dad talked for a few more minutes, and then Mark said, 'Follow me.'

They went down the corridor and out one of the doors to where all the other boys and girls were training outside. Mark introduced Cyril to all of the team. There were about twenty girls and boys in the athletics club. They were split up into groups and each group was doing different types of exercise. Mark put Cyril into one of the groups. Cyril was already really enjoying himself. Mark told his dad he could stay and watch, so his dad walked over and stood at the sideline watching his son.

Although Mark didn't allow Cyril to run because he didn't have the proper trainers, Cyril still had great fun doing all sorts of other exercises. He was made to feel so welcome.

No one said to him that he was too scrawny or that he would be no good. He only received encouragement from all the other boys and girls. One of the girls, Anne, said to him, 'I only started six weeks ago, and it's great.'

One of the boys said, 'We're going to try and get you on our relay team, Cyril. You have long legs. You should be able to run faster than the rest of us.'

Cyril laughed and said, 'I didn't know I had long legs.'

He made new friends that day and the coach said to him, 'You can come down every Monday, Wednesday and Saturday to begin with.' Turning to everyone, Coach Mark said, 'Off you all go, home now. See you Monday evening.'

Cyril asked Anne, 'What time Monday evening?' as they walked into the changing rooms.

'Six,' she said.

A few minutes later, they were all walking out the main door. All the boys and girls were so friendly.

His coach was standing at the gate. He said to Cyril, 'Looking forward to seeing you Monday evening.'

'Well, how did you enjoy your first training session?' asked Cyril's dad.

'It was great and I have made loads of new friends. Thanks, Dad, for staying and watching me.'

'What else would I be doing on a Saturday morning?'

Cyril was having such a good time chatting with his dad that he didn't even notice the journey home.

As they walked into the kitchen, his mum said, 'Well, tell me, how did it go?'

He told her all about the exercises he did and even gave her some demonstrations. He said, 'I wasn't allowed to run around the track but the coach, Mark, wants me down on a Monday and Wednesday evening at six o'clock and Saturday mornings at eleven o'clock, and we have a race on in two weeks' time. Coach Mark wants me to come to the race, even though I won't be running.' Cyril was so excited.

His dad said, 'Tomorrow, your mum is going to bring you shopping to get those trainers, and a T-shirt and shorts.' He rooted in his pocket, took out a piece of paper and handed it to Cyril's mum, saying, 'Coach Mark said these are the trainers we must get Cyril.'

His mum looked at the piece of paper and said, 'Actually, let's have lunch first and then why don't we all walk down to the sports shop together?'

Cyril's mum took all the ingredients for lunch out of the fridge: salad leaves, tomatoes, peppers, all kinds of things. His dad took the big bowl down from the top shelf. This was Cyril's dad's favourite meal to prepare. It was a little ritual and his dad was very proud of it, though Mum and Cyril always gave him a helping hand.

When lunch was ready, Cyril's dad gave a big smile and served up the salad on everyone's plate.

After lunch, there was a quick tidy-up and the kitchen was sparkling in no time.

Cyril walked down into town with his mum and dad, and they went into the local sports shop. Cyril had never been in a sports shop before. The walls of the shop were lined with trainers and boots of all kinds, and the shop was full of different types of tracksuits, shorts, T-shirts and protective gear.

The man in the sports shop took the piece of paper from Cyril's mum and walked down towards the back of the shop. The man made him try on three pairs of trainers until Cyril was sure they fitted him perfectly. He asked the man about some of the sports gear he saw hanging on racks. The man said that Cyril wouldn't need any of that equipment for running as it was protective gear for when playing football or hurling.

 After they bought his new trainers, Cyril's mum suggested they go to the second-hand shop to buy his T-shirts and shorts. She pointed out that it would be more eco-friendly than buying them from the sports shop. His mum found him a few pairs of shorts and a couple of T-shirts in the second-hand shop that were as good as new.

Cyril said, 'Thanks Mum and Dad for getting me my trainers, T-shirts and shorts.'

When they got home, he went upstairs and tried everything on. Then he went down to the front room to where his dad and mum were. His dad said, 'You look great, Cyril, just like an athlete.'

Cyril went back upstairs and changed his clothes again. He folded up the new T-shirts and shorts, and put them in a drawer. He put his trainers into the end of his wardrobe for safe-keeping.

When he went back downstairs, he said to his mum and dad, 'Is it okay for me to go out to meet my friends?'

His mum said, 'Yes, off you go, but be back in time for tea.'

As Cyril went out the back door, he shouted, 'I'm going to go down to Tommy's.'

'Okay,' said his dad.

Chapter 4

Cyril Cheering
on his Team

Cyril got down to his friend Tommy's house and knocked on the door. Tommy opened it. The first thing he said was, 'I saw you down at the sports club this morning.' Cyril explained that he had joined the running club and that his mum and dad had taken him into town that afternoon to buy trainers, shorts and T-shirts.

He said to Tommy, 'Can you come out for a little while?'

Tommy said, 'I have to mind my little sister. She wants to go to the playground.'

'I could help you mind your little sister?'

So the three of them walked over to the playground. A couple of hours later, as they walked back to Tommy's house, Cyril said, 'Playgrounds are actually great fun, and I enjoyed running after your little sister and taking turns with you to push her on the swing. I liked standing at the end of the slide waiting on her to come down.'

Tommy said, 'Well, it is exhausting. My little sister helps to keep me fit.' The two boys said goodbye at Tommy's house.

On Monday, when Cyril was getting ready to go down to the sports club, his mum said, 'I'll go down with you.'

But Cyril said to his mum, 'I'm meeting Tommy at his house. You don't need to come down to the sports club with me. Tommy is going to football now too. All the other boys and girls from running say they leave at half five as well, and they all usually bump into each other on the way down.'

His mum said, 'Are you sure?'

'Yes. Tommy leaves his house at half five, so I'll leave here at twenty past and then I'll walk down with Tommy and meet all the other boys and girls along the way. And I'll walk back home with Tommy too.'

Cyril enjoyed going to the running club to train, and on the days he wasn't there, he would do the shopping for his mum. She no longer even had to ask him to cut the grass. As soon as he saw it needed cutting, he did it, and all the weeding too.

Two weeks later, Mark started Cyril running on the track, but Cyril found it really hard. When walking back home, after he'd said goodbye to Tommy, he told his guardian angel what was on his mind. 'What's the point, Swift?' he said. 'I'm hopeless. I can't even run.'

His guardian angel whispered in his ear, 'I have a running angel running alongside you and in front of you at different times, giving you encouragement, so run and let your feet feel light. You are never last. Don't give up.'

'Okay,' said Cyril, 'but you will have to keep on encouraging me, Swift.'

At the next training session, Mark announced that other teams were going to be coming to their track on Saturday for racing, and he wanted everyone to do their best. He said to Cyril, 'I want you to watch every single race carefully, and remember to give our team lots of encouragement.'

Cyril said, 'Yes, I will cheer you all and be shouting at the top of my lungs.'

Cyril told his mum and dad that there would be races on Saturday. They said that they would be there cheering on his team too.

When Saturday morning came, as Cyril went out the back door, he said to his dad and mum, 'Don't forget. Don't be late. The first race is at eleven.'

'We'll be there,' Cyril's dad shouted after him.

Cyril met his friend Tommy as usual and they walked down to the sports club. Tommy was going to watch the races with Cyril before starting football practice. They arrived down there at nine o'clock that morning. The other boys and girls were there too. The first race was at eleven, so Mark was having them doing lots of exercises to warm up.

At about ten o'clock, lots of parents and supporters started to turn up at the sports club to watch the races. The car park was packed.

Cyril was standing to the right of the track. He spoke silently to his guardian angel and said, 'Swift, I wish I was racing with my team.'

His guardian angel put his arms around Cyril and said, 'Don't be disappointed. When the coach believes you're ready, he will let you race.'

But Cyril gave a sigh of disappointment and said, 'I know, but I wish I was ready now.'

'Well, when they're racing,' Swift said, 'imagine you're racing along with them.'

Just then, Cyril heard his mum and dad calling him and he turned around. They looked so excited about coming to watch the racing that they made him laugh. They came and stood beside him. Cyril told his dad and mum that the coach told him he was to watch every single race and, of course, cheer his team on. Cyril's mum handed him a bottle of water, some fruit and a bar of chocolate. Cyril said, 'Thanks, Mum. I am getting hungry now,' and he took a bite out of his apple.

When the racing began, Cyril did an awful lot of cheering. Sometimes, he was disappointed when his team did not win, but he did as his coach said and he watched all the runners carefully. His team did not win every race, but they did win some medals, and the coach was very proud of them. It was a great day. Cyril felt as if he had run the races himself and he was hoping that one day he too could win a medal, even just one.

Cyril said to his dad and mum, 'I'll be back in a few minutes. I just want to run into my team and tell them how great they were, and then, I'll be back out.'

His dad said, 'Take your time, Cyril.'

Cyril burst in through the door of the locker room. His teammates were holding the medals up. Mark turned round to Cyril and said, 'Get into this photo. You are a part of this team as well.'

Cyril felt so proud and one of the boys holding one of the medals took hold of Cyril's hand and the two of them held up one of the medals together, Cyril with a big smile on his face.

Just before they all left the locker room, Mark shouted, 'Lads, by the way, just because we won medals today doesn't mean you don't turn up on Monday evening for training.'

One of the girls, Mary, who was standing closest to Coach Mark, turned to him and said, 'You never let any of us miss training. Even the time I sprained my ankle, you still had me sitting down here on the bench, watching.'

Mark ignored her remark and said, 'Off you all go now and have fun.'

All the boys and girls said goodbye to Coach Mark and thanked him. One shouted, 'We wouldn't have won any medals if it wasn't for you Coach!'

Cyril's mum and dad were waiting outside. They were talking to the parents of some of the girls and boys on Cyril's team. One of the dads turned to Cyril and said, 'We've been hearing a lot about you and how hard you are working.'

Cyril said, 'Thanks!'

A few minutes later, he was walking home with his mum and dad.

CHAPTER 5

PREPARING TO RACE

One evening, Mark said, 'I'm going to put you into some practice races with your team, just to see how you do. I want you to push yourself, but I don't want you to overdo it.'

Cyril said, 'What do you mean?'

Mark said, 'You don't have to win. I just really want to see what distance you can go.'

So at each training session, Cyril's coach would have him race with four or five others from the team, or have him learning to take off from the starting line or even learning to pass a baton, which was tricky. Sometimes, he would miss it altogether and just make a mess of it.

Even though he never won any of the races, Mark seemed to be very pleased with Cyril's progress. But Cyril wasn't pleased. Most of the time he just couldn't keep up with the other runners. He always ended up last and that was really disappointing him.

His guardian angel was giving him as much encouragement as possible, whispering in Cyril's ear,

'Remember, I have a running angel with you, Cyril. Imagine your feet light like a feather as you run. As you did when you ran around the garden when you were only three. You were able to do it then. I know, Cyril, you can do it now.'

Cyril spoke to Swift silently in his mind: 'I'm not going to give up.'

After a few more weeks of training had passed, Cyril was getting really good at passing the baton and taking off correctly for a race, but he still wasn't winning any races. His guardian angel sometimes whispered to him, 'Don't be disappointed.'

Cyril would say he was disappointed that he could feel the strength draining out of him, and then Swift would say, 'Remember, it's not all about winning. It's about enjoying the sport, becoming part of it.'

'That's easy for you to say,' said Cyril in his mind as he was out on the track training. He often walked back into the changing room with the team, following the coach, feeling a bit frustrated with himself and wanting to do better.

Today in the changing room, he sat down on one of the benches and was rooting through his haversack when his guardian angel said to him, 'You have a running angel that is supporting you. Your running angel is always last because you always overtake your running angel.'

'Oh, really?' Cyril said out loud. One of the other boys in the changing room asked him, 'What did you say?'

'I said "ouch" because my feet feel a little sore.'

The boy said to him, 'Ask your mum or dad to give you a foot massage. By the way, my name is Daniel.'

'Mine's Cyril.'

'You're getting closer to us all when you are out on the track. You're going to catch up soon and overtake us all.'

Cyril was amazed at what Daniel was saying. 'Thanks,' he said. 'You really think so? Sometimes I feel like giving up.'

'I used to feel the same way myself,' said Daniel. 'I've been in this club for two years now and I can tell you, I was never as good as you in such a short space of time. Don't give up, Cyril. Our team needs you.'

'Thanks,' he said to Daniel. 'I won't give up. I'll keep on trying and do my best.'

The boys and girls of the team walked home together. Tommy was there too because he had stayed after football to watch. Every so often, one of them would wave goodbye as they peeled off to head home. Eventually,

Tommy and Cyril were left to walk the final part of the way together. Sometimes, that part of the walk home took much longer because Tommy and Cyril would stop and go into the shop and buy some sweets. They had become best friends. Afterwards they waved good-bye to each other and said, 'See you tomorrow.'

Cyril had only a short distance to go on his own. It only took him a few minutes these days as he would jog the rest of the way home. This time, as he did, he said, 'Thanks, Swift, for encouraging me,' to his guardian angel.

When his house came into view, Cyril said, 'By the way Swift, thank you for the running angel. Now I know the angel is running in front of me and I must overtake it, and I'll try to do that every single time and try to get faster. I do love running.'

Every time Cyril was down at the club, his coach would have him practising racing with the best runners on the team. And that was usually after an hour of exercise.

On this particular evening, Cyril ran out onto the track with his friend Daniel and some of the others. When he felt one of his trainers wasn't on properly, he walked over to one of the benches on the side of the track and sat down. He took off his trainer. There was a little stone in it and his sock was a little twisted. As he sat there fixing his trainer and sock, his guardian angel whispered in his ear, 'When you are running, today with the other boys and girls, remember the running angel is in front of you and you have to overtake it.'

Daniel called him and told him to hurry up.

A few seconds later, Cyril was up on his feet and running over to Daniel and the others. He joined in the warm-up that Coach Mark was leading.

After they'd all run around the track four times, Mark got them to line up in rows of five, giving each row a different exercise to do at the same time. Then he called Cyril to one side and said to him, 'I want you to run round the track twice on your own.' This was the first time Coach Mark had ever asked him to do anything on his own. Cyril got into position and Mark counted to three, and then Cyril started to run. Coach Mark was timing him on his stopwatch. When Cyril passed Coach Mark on his first lap, his coach shouted at him, 'Very good, Cyril. Keep running.'

'Your running angel is running in front of you,' Swift whispered in his ear. 'See if you can overtake it.'

Cyril built up speed and imagined the running angel in front of him. He concentrated hard and tried to overtake it. He didn't notice he had run past Mark until he heard his coach shouting at him to stop. Cyril stopped and jogged slowly back to Mark. 'That's the best run you've ever done, Cyril. Keep warm there now. I'm going to put you in a race with some of the others.'

Cyril trying to catch up and pass out his running angel.

A few minutes later, Coach Mark put four boys and two girls into a hundred-metre race with Cyril. They got into position and when Mark counted to three, they all ran. Cyril remembered his running angel. One of the girls and one of the boys were running beside him, but the other four were well ahead. But Cyril was concentrating on seeing in his mind the running angel ahead of him, and he ran harder and harder to catch up with it. Without noticing, he overtook all the children ahead of him. He passed the finishing line and realised – he had won! All the others in the team came over to congratulate him.

Daniel had come in second. 'I told you you would beat us one day. Well done, Cyril.'

Mark said to him, 'Well done, Cyril. I knew you could do it with those long legs of yours.'

Every day after that, Cyril raced with the team. Sometimes he didn't win, but a lot of the time he did.

Some of the other running teams from other areas were starting to come to the sports club to practise too, because it had such a good running track, and one Saturday morning, Coach Mark said to the team, 'I've had a talk with the coaches of the other teams that are coming to practise and we're going to have some mixed races.'

The boys and girls were a bit shocked. They said, 'But Coach, what if we're no good?'

'You will learn a lot from the other teams, even watching them, and racing with them will give you more encouragement. I believe it will be good for all of you. You are all good runners.' Mark hesitated for a moment and then he spoke again. 'I hope you are enjoying it. Have fun as well. You must enjoy your sport. You must get pleasure out of it because that's what makes it worthwhile, and then if you win a medal, that's a bonus. Now, get your gear on and let's go.'

After their warm-up and races with the other teams, Daniel said to Cyril, 'This is not bad. I like it. No pressure on.'

'I do too,' said Cyril. 'Some of those other lads are very nice. I haven't won a real race yet but I guess I will soon.'

Daniel said, 'You will Cyril, have no doubt about that.'

A week later, Cyril was on the starting line, practising with a few members of the other teams, when his guardian angel whispered in his ear, 'Remember, Cyril, the running angel is in front of you already. Let your feet be light and overtake your running angel.'

When they started to run, he thought only about his running angel, and soon enough he had overtaken some of the other runners. He didn't get to the finishing line first, but he did finish third. He was very happy and so were his team.

Back in the locker room, Mark said, 'The first official big race is next Saturday and I want everyone down at the club every evening from five o'clock for practice. Today was your last day training with the other teams.'

All the team felt a little bit disappointed but also very excited about the big race on Saturday. The coach told each and every one of them which race they would be running in. Cyril couldn't wait to get home to tell his parents.

As Tommy and Cyril walked the last stretch to Tommy's house, all they talked about was Cyril's first race on Saturday. Cyril said to Tommy, 'If any of us win a race or even get third place, it means we might qualify for the final.' He was very excited.

As they reached his estate, Tommy said, 'Goodbye. See you tomorrow.' Cyril waved goodbye to his friend and jogged the rest of the way home.

He was dying to tell his mum and dad the great news about his first official race, but when he reached the house, the car wasn't there. He was a little disappointed and walked in the back door. Nobody was at home. There was a note on the table. Mum and Dad had decided to drive down to the park and go for a walk. They would be back later.

It was an hour later when Cyril heard the car. He ran down the stairs and opened the hall door. His mum said, 'What's up?'

With great excitement, Cyril told them about the race on Saturday.

'Great, son,' said his dad as they walked into the house. 'We'll be there and we'll cheer you on.'

Cyril's mum put the kettle on and made some tea. Cyril couldn't stop talking. 'Coach Mark says I'm ready. I don't want to let the team down. I'm going to do my best.'

His dad said, 'That's all you can do – just your best. Is your whole team going to be racing?'

Cyril said, 'Yes, but in different races. I'm in the same race as Daniel. I hope one of us wins a medal. Coach Mark said we need to be down at the sports centre at five o'clock every evening this week for practice.'

'First thing you need to do,' said Cyril's mum, 'is calm down a little, and you're going to have to eat well.'

'You mean all that *healthy* food?' said Cyril.

Cyril's mum said, 'Yes, food that will give you plenty of energy and keep you going for the week, but especially Saturday, so you have to be home for every meal and not eating loads of junk in between.'

'Okay then.'

'And I'm sure your coach said you will need your rest too,' said his dad.

'I get the hint,' said Cyril, and he said goodnight to his mum and dad and went off to bed.

That night Cyril dreamed of running on Saturday in the race and winning. In his dream, he could see the running angel in front of him, moving fast, and he was catching it up and overtaking it. He won the race and he could hear everyone cheering.

CHAPTER 6

CYRIL'S FIRST RACE

At breakfast, Cyril told his mum and dad that he had been dreaming that he had won the race on Saturday. 'I know it was only a dream,' he said, 'but maybe I can do it.'

His mum and dad said, 'Yes, maybe you can.'

Every evening that week, the team was down at the track practising. They worked very hard, just as they had worked very hard all through the summer. Then before they knew it, it was Friday. They were all beginning to get a little nervous, but Coach Mark told them not to worry – they were the best team he'd ever had and he hoped he would have them next year as well. He told them they should go straight home and go to bed and have a good rest, as they needed to be down at the sports centre at nine o'clock on the dot the next morning.

Cyril had the same dream again that night. He saw his running angel running in front of him, and he ran faster and faster until eventually he passed the angel and won the race.

At half seven on Saturday morning, Cyril's mum called him for breakfast. She gave him a good, hearty breakfast, and she said, 'It will give you plenty of energy.'

Cyril's dad walked into the kitchen and sat down at the breakfast table. 'Good morning, Cyril,' he said. 'I can't wait to see you racing in the big race. I know you will do great, son. What time do you think we should go down?'

'The first race starts at half ten,' said Cyril, 'so you better be down about ten o'clock, so you can get a place and I can hear you both cheering me and the team on.'

'Don't worry, son,' said his dad, 'we'll be there. I can give you a lift down?'

'No, I'd rather walk. Coach Mark said walking down to the sports centre would help to warm us up for the race.'

'Okay,' said his dad.

Cyril left the house about half eight. As he went out the back door, his mum said, 'Enjoy the race. See you soon.'

Cyril shouted, 'Thanks, Mum,' as he ran out the gate and down to meet Tommy, who was standing at the corner waiting for him. Tommy was waving at Cyril, saying, 'Hurry up! You'll be late.'

On the way, they met the rest of the team. There was great excitement.

When they reached the sports fields, Tommy said, 'See you later. Good luck!'

Coach Mark was already in the locker room, waiting for the team. He gave his usual lecture, encouraging them. He said again how proud he was of them and asked them to do their best. That's all he expected from them, he said. But of course the team always wanted to do one million times better then Coach Mark ever hoped for. Then he had them all wish each other the best of luck. He told them all to support each other. They all gave three cheers and suddenly they were out on the track to warm up. They saw all of the other teams there too.

At ten o'clock, the crowds were already starting to arrive. The team were told to head back into the locker room.

As they were walking back, Cyril glanced around to see if he could see his mum or dad. Just as he was about to give up, he saw the two of them standing at the left-hand corner of the track, not too far from the starting line. He saw Tommy there too with his friends. They were all waving to him and he waved back.

He went into the locker room with the rest of the team and started to get ready. His guardian angel whispered in his ear, 'Remember, Cyril, your running angel is running in front of you. Catch up with your running angel and overtake it.'

He spoke back to Swift, in his own mind, saying, 'I'm not going to forget about my running angel. I have been dreaming about it all week, running in front of me in my big race and me catching him up and overtaking my running angel and winning the race. I'm going to imagine the running angel in front of me all of the time.'

Mark said, 'Okay, first race is at half ten.' He called out the names for each race and told those boys and girls to stay together, so no one got mixed up.

Daniel said, 'Coach, I'm in two races.'

Coach Mark said, 'Yes, and so is everyone. All the team are going to be in two different races. Racing is going on the whole day. Daniel and Cyril, you are running at one o'clock, and then three o'clock. Everyone look at your card. Don't get mixed up with your times. If you're in doubt, come to me. We don't want anyone racing in the wrong race.'

Cyril said, 'What do we do in the meantime?'

'You rest and warm up and you help your teammates who are in the races before you.'

'Okay, Coach!'

Mark said, 'Now, a quick warm-up for those racing in the first race.'

He took that part of the team and went out onto the pitch with them.

The rest of the team watched from the sidelines, though they didn't stand still. They were jumping about, making sure that they stayed loose as well as cheering their teammates on.

In the first race, one of the team finished in third place. They were very happy. As the day wore on the team won a few medals and in no time at all, it was time for Daniel and Cyril to run their first race.

They went outside with Coach Mark. They nodded to the other racers as they got into position. Standing there, Cyril imagined the running angel in front of him, standing in position as well. When the gun was fired, Cyril ran as fast as he could, determined to pass the running angel. He was so focused that he didn't even hear the cheers from the crowds. He just imagined himself running past the angel, and then all of a sudden, he was crossing the finishing line.

Cyril didn't realise he had won the race until everyone started to congratulate him. Swift whispered in his ear, 'Well done, you imagined your feet light and you were able to catch up and pass the running angel you saw in front of you. Congratulations, Cyril.'

Daniel and Cyril held hands and jumped

around. Cyril had won and Daniel had finished third. Mark said, 'Well done, lads.'

Cyril's mum and dad found their way around the track to him. His mum said to Cyril, 'You ran so fast! I couldn't believe it.'

His dad said, 'Well, he's my son. Of course he can run fast.'

'You can't run at all,' his mum retorted, and they both laughed.

His dad said, 'Cyril, your mum and I are so proud of you.'

Cyril said, 'I have to go now,' as all the team were heading back into the locker room.

Some of the team were racing at two o'clock or at half two for their second race. It was only then back in the locker room that it dawned on Cyril that he had another race at three o'clock. He looked at Daniel and said, 'I forgot we have another race at three.'

Daniel said, 'Yeah, so we have to keep moving so our legs won't stiffen up. Let's go to the canteen and get something to eat.'

Mark shouted after them, 'Only something small. You don't want to get cramp pains either.'

'Okay, Coach,' they shouted back. They both had a snack and a drink and then went back to the changing room to help their teammates who were racing next.

Before Cyril and Daniel knew it, it was time for their own second race. Coach Mark went out with them. He wished Daniel and Cyril the best of luck and said, 'Just do your best, lads. That's all.'

When Cyril was standing there in position again, he imagined the running angel in front of him in position too, ready to run. Then the gun was fired, and Cyril ran as fast as he could. He let his feet feel light like a feather, and tried to overtake the angel. In the next moment, the race was over and again, everyone was cheering. He couldn't believe it. He had won again, and his friend Daniel had finished second this time.

The three medal winners high-fived and congratulated each other.

There were still two more races to go, so they all headed back into the locker room with Mark to cool down and to give encouragement to their teammates who were running in the last two races. Then they all went back outside to cheer them on.

When the last race was over, back in the changing room, Coach Mark said to all the team, 'This was the best year I've ever had with any team. Congratulations! In every race, someone from the team won a medal. It's all about supporting each other when you're racing and doing your best.' He had such a big smile on his face.

The three children celebrating their medals, with Cyril
in first place and Daniel in second. They have feathers,
signs of their guardian angels, all around them.

They went outside to be presented with their medals. The winners for each race stood together holding hands high in the air. Cyril couldn't believe he had won two medals and a cup for best beginner. His mum said, 'We'll have to do something special tonight. Let's all go out for dinner.'

Cyril said, 'That would be great.' Then he asked his

mum and dad, 'Would it be okay for me to walk home with Tommy?'

They said, 'Yes.'

Most of the team walked home that day. They were all so excited on their walk back. After a little while, they parted ways as usual and Cyril said goodbye to Tommy at his house.

On the last stretch of his journey home, Cyril had an opportunity to talk to his guardian angel. He looked around and saw that there was no one else on the road, so he spoke quietly to Swift. 'Thank you, Swift. You are the best guardian angel any young boy could have and I know all my friends have guardian angels too. Thank you for putting the running angel in front of me and telling me to imagine the running angel running ahead of me all of the time and that I was to catch it up on it and overtake the running angel. I will do that in every race that I run. Thank you, guardian angel, Swift.'

'Well done Cyril,' Swift replied. 'Now, go into the house and go out for dinner with your mum and dad. You have something to celebrate.'

'Thank you,' Cyril said again, just as his mum and dad drove in past the gate.

Miley and his Friends

CHAPTER 1

MILEY'S IDEA

Miley's guardian angel reminded him that when he was six months old, he used to always pull at the buttons on his granny's cardigan. 'I used to whisper in your ear, Miley, that my name is Big Buttons.'

Miley started to laugh. 'I do love your name. Did I say Big Buttons in baby language when I was small? Did I?'

Miley's guardian angel said, 'Yes, but now you just call me Buttons. I do love the way you still wear buttons for me. You always have big buttons on your sleeves.'

Miley's mum called up the stairs: 'Hurry down, Miley. I have a job for you.'

'Okay,' Miley called back.

Just as Miley was going to go down the stairs, his guardian angel whispered in his ear, 'What about your teeth?'

'Thank you, Buttons,' replied Miley as he pushed open the bathroom door to get his toothpaste and toothbrush. He brushed his teeth, washed his face and his hands and then ran down the stairs. As he did, he said to Buttons, 'This morning, I feel very grown up. I'm nine years old,' and when he got to the end of the stairs, he turned and looked at his guardian angel with a big smile on his face.

Miley's mum asked him to go out into the garden to look for anything that they might be able to use for a Christmas wreath. 'Okay,' said Miley as he opened the back door and closed it behind him.

Miley stood in the centre of the garden, looking around to see if there was anything that would do. He couldn't see anything for the wreath. He started to walk back towards the back door of his house, and while he was kicking some leaves that were on the ground, he said to his guardian angel, 'Why don't you help me? I don't see anything in the garden that would be of any use. Buttons, Mum would be so disappointed if I don't find something.'

Buttons whispered in his ear, 'Look to the left and over near the wall. I see some funny shaped twigs. A few of them still have some beautiful green leaves attached.'

'Thanks,' said Miley, and he ran over to where they were on the ground and gathered up the twigs. He started to count them. There were six, with the odd green leaf here and there. Miley felt happy.

Miley spoke to his guardian angel and said, 'I think Mum will get some great ideas. She can attach some lovely things in between the green leaves. Thank you, Buttons.'

Miley turned around with his arms full and headed for the back door. When he got there, he kicked the door with his foot and called his mum to open it.

When his mum opened the door, Miley said, 'Look what I have!'

She was delighted. 'Where did you find them?'

'Over by the wall,' Miley said.

His mum said, 'I don't know how I missed them. I searched the garden this morning from top to bottom.'

'Well, Mum, my guardian angel told me to look to my left, and that's when I saw them.'

'Did you thank your guardian angel, Miley?'

'Yes, of course I did, Mum. Where should I put them?'

'Over there, on the table in the corner of the room. That would be the best place for them for now as I'm not ready to make the Christmas wreath yet. We will need a lot more things.'

As Miley put the twigs on the table, he said to his mum, 'They are funny shaped.'

'Yes,' she said, 'they are definitely funny-shaped twigs and very beautiful.'

He looked up at her face and thought she looked a little worried. 'Don't worry, Mum. You always get great ideas at Christmas time, and I will make a Christmas card for Granny and Grandda.'

Miley's mum said, 'You can do that tomorrow.'

Miley sat up at the kitchen table as his mum handed him a sandwich and a glass of milk. 'I still have plenty of time before school,' he said. 'Could you tell me the Christmas story? You make it more interesting than they do in school.'

His mum sat at the table with a cup of tea in her hands and told him the story about the little baby named Jesus who was born in a stable and how little they had. She went on to tell him about the shepherds bringing the lambs as a gift and, of course, the three wise men. Miley was fascinated. This story always touched his heart. He loved to hear it. Strangers bringing gifts to this family who were poor and lived in a stable, and the shepherds bringing gifts of lambs from their flock of sheep to the family. This part of the story fascinated Miley. He said to his mum, 'This stable must've had other animals like horses and donkeys and camels. I can imagine all the animals that must've come to visit the little baby and his mum and dad too.'

She agreed, 'I'm sure there were lots of animals. Maybe there was a fox there too, and a rabbit.'

Miley said, 'And probably plenty of birds as well up in the rafters. And maybe some mice there too, Mum. I heard mice live in stables as well as houses.'

His mum laughed. 'We have no mice in this house.'

Miley asked, 'Why did all those animals go to the stable?'

'They came because this little baby was born and the stable was full of angels. They helped to keep the stable warm. The three wise men were the last to arrive,' his mum said. 'They were the kings bringing expensive and precious gifts for the little baby.'

Miley said to his mum, 'But the wise men and shepherds didn't even know who this family was, and yet they brought these gifts. I do love that about Christmas, Mum. I love getting gifts because I'm a child and everyone tries to give gifts to children at Christmas, and in school, we do something special for children in other parts of the world who don't have anybody to give them a gift. We fill a box with nice things.'

Miley's mum said to him, 'That's important.'

Then Buttons whispered in his ear, 'Sharing is caring, Miley.'

Miley's mum said, 'You have to remember, the holy family didn't have much but they did have each other. Just like you and me, and your granny and grandda. We have each other.'

'And don't forget about our guardian angels too, Mum. We have them to help us,' Miley said as he turned around and gave her a hug.

Just as he was going out the hall door, he wondered if there was something special he could do for Christmas. As he waved goodbye to his mum, his guardian angel said to him: 'Yes, there is something you can do. I will put the thought into your head, Miley.'

He replied to Buttons, 'Don't distract me too much when I'm in school though, otherwise the teacher will give out because I'm not paying attention.'

As he walked down to school, which took about ten minutes, his guardian angel whispered in his ear, 'You could give a gift to nature for looking after baby Jesus when he was a little baby, comforting him and keeping him warm.'

'I never thought of giving back a present to nature for helping the baby Jesus. Buttons, that is a great idea,' said Miley. 'We always forget about the animals don't we?' he continued. 'But what can I do?'

'Talk to your friends Robert and Lacey when you're walking back home from school. Ask them what are they doing at this time of the year? They know you celebrate Christmas and I know they will want to play a part. Perhaps you can all come up with an idea together.'

'Okay,' said Miley.

Just as he got to the school entrance, Miley, forgetting where he was, spoke loudly: 'Don't distract me now, Buttons. I don't want my teacher to give out to me.'

Three other boys came up behind Miley and one said, 'You're talking to yourself again.'

'No,' said Miley to the boys, 'just focusing on our exam today in English.' He gave the three boys a smile.

'Whoops, we forgot about that exam this morning,' and the two boys rushed past Miley, walking fast down the corridor as nobody was allowed to run. Miley went into his class happily and gave his friend, Robert, an especially big smile. Robert was Miley's best friend. Miley liked school, but most of all, he loved break time when they could be out in the yard playing. He liked sports as well.

Miley was good at most of the subjects in school, and sometimes he would help Robert, who had difficulty with maths. This would happen during lunch break. They'd sit on a little wall, and Robert would ask Miley about some of the things he couldn't quite grasp. Miley would help him by explaining them.

Miley's guardian angel had told him when Robert came to the school as a new pupil that Robert would end up being one of his best friends.

Miley had found it hard to make friends with the boys and girls in his school. Then one day at lunch, Buttons gave him the courage to go up to Robert and talk to him. From that day on, they became best friends, and Miley's guardian angel told him to always keep a piece of paper and a pencil in his pocket, so that he could help Robert with his maths whenever needed.

As Miley and Robert sat on the wall, eating their lunch, Robert said to Miley, 'Can you help me with those new division problems we're doing before we go back to class?' Miley took his pencil and paper out of his pocket and began to explain the problems to Robert.

A few minutes later, Miley put the pencil and paper back into his pocket and asked Robert, 'Do you understand now?'

Robert said, 'Yes.'

'By the way, I have a plan,' said Miley, 'and when we are walking home from school, I want us to talk about it. Hopefully we will meet Lacey. We can hang around for her on the green if she's a bit late getting out of her school.'

Robert said, 'I'm dying to know your plan. What is it? What are you up to, Miley?'

Just then the school bell rang, and Miley said, 'You have to wait. Let's get back into class.'

Just before the end of the school day, the teacher reminded them that there were only two weeks left until the Christmas holidays, and also that they would have a spelling test on Friday.

Then the bell rang and all of the children stood up and said, 'Thank you, Teacher. We will see you tomorrow.' They packed their bags, got their jackets and headed out of school.

As they walked across the schoolyard, Robert said to Miley, 'Tell me about your plan.'

Miley said, 'No, not yet. Wait till we get out of school and across the road.'

Just then, Lacey came running up to them shouting, 'Wait for me.'

Robert said to her, 'We always wait for you at the park.'

'I was first out of my class today. My guardian angel told me to hurry,' said Lacey.

'We are heading up to the park now,' said Robert. 'Miley has a plan and he won't tell us till we get there.'

Lacey's eyes grew big and focused on Miley. She said, 'What's the plan, Miley? I'm dying to hear.'

'Let's get to the green first,' said Miley.

So they walked fast and in a couple of minutes, they were there. They all sat down on the grass.

Miley said to Robert and Lacey, 'You know I'm a Christian, and that I celebrate Christmas? It's about the little baby being born named Jesus and his parents.'

Robert and Lacey both said, 'Yes.'

Miley said, 'I know you, Robert, are Jewish and Lacey, you're Muslim.'

Robert said, 'But what has this got to do with your plan Miley?'

Miley said, 'We always talk about our guardian angels.'

'And we ask our guardian angels to help us every day, and they do,' said Robert. Then he said, 'We are all aware of Christmas time even though my mum and dad don't celebrate it. We celebrate Hanukkah, which is around Christmas time too, and I like to share the celebration of Christmas as well. So what's your plan, Miley? Has it to do with Christmas?'

'Yes,' he said. 'My guardian angel put the thought into my mind when he whispered in my ear.'

'You mean Buttons,' said Lacey. 'Don't forget to use the name of your guardian angel.'

Miley laughed. 'Thanks, Lacey, for reminding me,' he said with a big smile on his face. 'At Christmas time, we give presents to each other and we try to help people all over the world. We think of others, just like the shepherds and the three wise men, but Buttons reminded me about the animals, and said that it would be nice to give nature a gift at Christmas. I want you to help me come up with a plan, so we can thank nature – like thanking the animals in the stable that kept baby Jesus warm and comforted him.'

Lacey said, 'Even though I don't celebrate Christmas, I am very aware of it and I know about the shepherds bringing the lambs and the wise men bringing gifts. I know about the angels telling these wise men, the strangers, to give precious gifts to an infant and its parents when they did not even know them. That is something I find very kind.'

Miley said, 'Yes, but we never think about nature that played a huge part in looking after the little family in the stable.'

The three of them stood there in the park. There was a little stream with trees and bushes surrounding it. There was a lot of rubbish in and around the bushes and in the shallow parts of the stream. As they stood there, their guardian angels spoke to them at the same time:

'The three of you could do something special here as a gift this Christmas to nature.'

Miley spoke first: 'My guardian angel, Buttons, said the three of us could do something special as our gift to nature.'

'That's exactly what my guardian angel said,' said Lacey.

'Mine as well,' said Robert.

'What could we do?' said Miley.

The three of them looked again at the little stream and the rubbish that was in and around the water.

Buttons whispered in his ear: 'Maybe you could clean up the mess around the stream. And you could make some little birdhouses and put them on the trees. Perhaps you could make a table as well, and use it to feed the birds every morning on the way to school – and on Christmas morning.'

'Buttons gave me a great idea,' said Miley. 'We could start by cleaning up this mess.'

Lacey said, 'Miley, but how can we clean the place up when we always have to go straight home from school? If I'm not home by a certain time, I get into trouble because Mam and Dad worry about me.'

'I'm the same,' Miley said.

'My dad gets very cross about if I'm not home on time to do my chores,' Robert said. 'What about

Saturday morning? Our parents know that we always meet on a Saturday morning.'

Miley said, 'Buttons also suggested we make bird boxes and a table to put seed on.'

'That's impossible,' said Robert. 'We would need help doing all of that. How can *we* make those things?'

Just then, Buttons whispered in Miley's ear: 'Do not worry.'

'Buttons said we're not to worry about that now,' Miley said. 'Somehow, we'll get the help, but I better head home now. The three of us better. We'll be late.'

The three of them continued walking, and talked about the things they might need to bring with them on Saturday, like gloves and bags. Just before the three best friends separated to go home, Miley said, 'Robert, Lacey, should we keep this a secret for now? If we tell our parents, they might not allow us to do it, or they might even try to take it over, and I'd like it to be our special project. We should gather our gloves and bags – whatever we think we will need – and hide them. I know I can put some things in the shed in the back garden.'

Lacey said, 'On Saturday morning, I can empty my haversack and put what I need into it.'

Robert said, 'I can do the same.'

The three of them said goodbye a few minutes later. 'See you at school tomorrow,' Miley shouted to his best friends as he walked away.

Miley was very excited and happy. 'I think God will be very happy with this Christmas present,' he said to his guardian angel. 'Do you, Buttons?'

His guardian angel said, 'Yes.'

CHAPTER 2

PREPARING FOR SATURDAY

When Miley got home from school, he went in the side gate of the house and headed straight round the back. There he saw his mum, out working in the garden. Miley dropped his schoolbag on the ground and ran to help his mum, going to the shed and getting the other rake so he could help rake up the leaves. Miley and his mum talked and when they had the leaves in a big pile, Miley picked up a handful and threw them at his mum. They had a leaf battle, throwing them at each other and kicking the leaves into the air, laughing and running in circles.

When they had finished having fun, they stopped and looked at each other, still laughing, and then looked around. They saw the leaves were scattered all over the garden again. That only made them laugh more. Miley said to his mum, 'Let's start raking all these leaves up again.'

She said, 'Let's rake the leaves over into the corner. This time, when it's done, we can't start throwing the leaves around the garden again or we will never get the job done.'

Miley just laughed, but his mum said, 'Now, I'm serious, Miley,' laughing back at him.

When they were finished, Miley said to his mum, 'I'll put the rakes into the shed.'

His mum went into the house. Miley picked up both of the rakes and dragged them behind him over to the shed. Just as he opened the shed door, Buttons whispered in his ear, 'Miley, this is an opportunity to see what you can take with you on Saturday.'

'Thanks,' said Miley to Buttons as he looked around the shed. He found a pair of gloves. He gave them a good shake to make sure there were no spiders in them. There were also some woven sacks at the back of the shed. He said to Buttons, 'Maybe these would be good for putting some of the rubbish into?' Miley rolled up the two sacks tightly and put them with the gloves on the shelf in the shed. He said to Buttons, 'I can grab them on Saturday morning when I'm going to meet Robert and Lacey.'

Buttons said to Miley, 'Don't forget your rake. You can put it near the back garden gate. You don't have to hide it from your mum.'

Miley took the rake. It was the one he used all the time, and it was a bit smaller than his mum's. As he stood at the back garden gate, looking around, he said to Buttons, 'I can see now where I can hide it. I can lay it on the ground just behind the bins. Mum won't see it there.'

Buttons said again, 'You don't have to hide it, Miley. You can tell your mum.'

Miley just ignored him.

Miley and his friends couldn't wait for Saturday to come. At first they thought the school week would never end, but Friday came quick enough.

On Friday at lunch break, while eating their lunch on the little wall in the schoolyard, Miley and Robert tested each other on spellings for their English test.

Then two other boys, James and Shane, came over to Miley and said to him, 'I see you have a friend now?'

Miley stood up and said, 'Do you mean Robert?'

The two boys didn't answer. Miley just stood there, looking at them.

Then, one of them reached out to give Miley a little push on his shoulder and said, 'What are you talking about?'

As they looked at Miley and Robert disdainfully, Robert stood up, giving Miley support.

Miley's guardian angel, Buttons, whispered in Miley's ear, 'Say nothing, just stare back.'

Miley staring back at James and Shane,
with Buttons giving him encouragement.

Miley did as Buttons said and a moment later, the two boys walked away.

'My legs turned to jelly,' Robert said as he sat back down on the wall.

Miley took a deep breath and sat back down beside Robert, who said, 'I don't really like those two boys. They are bullies.'

Miley's guardian angel whispered something in his ear, then Miley said, 'Buttons said they are only trying to be tough, showing off. Don't worry about them.'

The bell rang and Miley said to Robert, 'Let's get back to class.' As they walked across the schoolyard, they were both a little anxious about their spelling test. Miley said, 'Don't forget to ask your guardian angel to give you a helping hand with your test. I know you will get them all correct. You're great at spelling, Robert.'

Robert said, 'You too, Miley.'

Back in class, when they were sitting at their desks, their teacher said, 'Quiet down, boys. I'm not going to give you a spelling test just yet. It will be the last subject before class is over for the weekend. We are going to do some history first.'

There was a big sound of disappointment from all of the boys and girls in the class. But in no time at all, they were doing the spelling test and then, class was over.

Lacey was already at the school gate waiting on Miley and Robert. She was full of excitement so she had left school really quickly to meet the boys. She said to Miley as they walked home from school, 'What time will we meet tomorrow morning?'

'Ten o'clock,' said Miley.

When they got to the green where the little stream was, they had another good look around. As they walked across the green towards the stream, Miley said, 'I don't think we'll be able to get the whole place cleaned up just by ourselves, but we will do our best.'

Lacey said, 'Remember, it was your idea, Miley. I know Buttons put it into your head for a reason. I have my things in my haversack under my bed already. I have borrowed my mum's gardening gloves and my mum's hand cutters, which she uses on the rosebushes. I'm looking forward to tomorrow morning.' Just then, Lacey gave Robert a light dig in the ribs with her elbow, with a smile on her face.

Robert frowned at her for elbowing him, but then he said, 'Yes, I'm looking forward to tomorrow morning as well. I know where my dad's old gloves are. I know they will be big for me, but they will do the job. He got a new pair a few weeks ago.'

Miley said to Robert, 'Does that mean your dad is going to do some gardening this weekend?'

'I don't think so,' said Robert. 'He's painting the kitchen.'

Miley said, 'How are you going to sneak out the garden rake tomorrow?'

Robert laughed and said, 'I already have it hidden behind the brush at the back garden gate.'

Miley laughed too, and said, 'I hid my rake behind the bins at the back garden gate as well.'

Lacey started to laugh too but said instead, 'I don't have a rake.'

Miley and Robert said, 'That's okay. Two rakes will be enough.'

The three friends said goodbye and, heading home, went their separate ways.

When Miley walked in the back door, his mum said to him, 'You look very happy. Did you have a good day at school?'

'Yeah, I did.'

'What about your spelling test?' asked his mum. 'Did you get them all correct?'

'The teacher said she'd let us know on Monday,' he said as he sat up at the table.

She gave him a smile.

'Can I go around to Granny's house now instead of tomorrow morning?' Miley said.

Miley's mum asked, 'Why?'

'My friends and I have decided to meet at ten o'clock tomorrow.'

'That's early,' said Miley's mum. 'It's usually eleven.'

Buttons whispered in Miley's ear, 'You could tell your mum about the clean-up now.'

But Miley ignored Buttons' suggestion, and said, 'I love hanging around with Robert and Lacey at the weekend. You know, they are my best friends Mum. They are my only friends – as well as Buttons, my guardian angel, of course.'

'Okay,' she said. 'I got your granny's shopping this morning. Those two shopping bags by the door. Do you think you can manage them on your own?'

'Yes,' said Miley. 'I'm strong.' As he picked up the two shopping bags, he gave his mum a big smile and headed towards his grandmother's house, only three doors up the road.

When he reached his grandmother's, he went around the back to the garden gate. He put the two shopping bags down so he could put his hand through the opening in the gate and pull the latch across to let it swing open. He walked to the back door and kicked on it gently, because his hands were full. His grandmother opened the door and said, 'Oh my goodness, Miley, come in.' She reached down to help Miley with the shopping bags.

Then he helped his granny put the shopping away. 'Granny, is there anything else you need?' he asked.

She said, 'I would love you to come for a walk with me around the garden and tell me all about your friends.'

*Miley walking with his granny in her garden,
with the light of their guardian angels behind them.*

Miley and his granny walked around the garden, talking about nature and about Robert and Lacey.

Miley's granny said to him, 'If tomorrow is a nice sunny day, I might go for a walk across to the green, and then I will see you and your friends. Are you looking forward to Christmas?'

Miley said, 'Yes, I love Christmas.'

When they were back in the house, Miley's granny said, 'Your mum will be looking for you. It's getting late.'

He gave his granny a hug and said goodbye. It only took a few seconds to get back home.

Miley's mum said, 'Did you have a nice time visiting you granny on your own?'

'Yes,' said Miley. 'It was nice, just the two of us.'

His mum said, 'I have never seen you eat your dinner so quick.'

'I just want to get to bed early,' he said. 'I don't want to sleep in late in the morning. Mum, can I bring the clock up to my bedroom? Could you set the alarm for nine so I can have breakfast? And can I make my breakfast myself?'

Miley's mum said, 'Okay, I might have a lie-in in the morning.'

As Miley was getting into bed, he said to Buttons, 'I want to fall asleep straight away. I can't wait for tomorrow to come.' As soon as Miley's head touched the pillow, he fell asleep.

CHAPTER 3

A PRESENT FOR NATURE

The alarm rang and Miley woke up. He got dressed quickly, hurried into the bathroom, brushed his teeth and threw water on his face.

As he was heading down the stairs, Buttons said, 'Slow down. You will wake your mum.'

So every step Miley took after that towards the kitchen, he took as quietly as he could. He made himself a sandwich of peanut butter and jelly and poured himself out a glass of milk. It was quarter to ten.

Miley opened the back door and closed it gently. He went out to the shed to get the gloves and the sacks. He put them into his bag and took the rake out from behind the bins.

As he went through the garden gate, Buttons said to Miley, 'Don't forget to close it.' Miley put everything down on the ground. Buttons said to him, 'I think I will get lots of angels to give the three of you a helping hand.'

Miley said, 'That would be a good idea.'

When he got to the green, Robert and Lacey were already there. They shouted at him to hurry up. He ran over. Robert and Lacey said together, 'Where should we start?'

'Let's pick up all the rubbish first,' said Miley. 'I have some bags.'

'I have some too,' Lacey said.

'I think we have to use the rakes to get some of the papers and cans and bottles out from among the bushes,' Robert added.

'Miley, remind them to put the gloves on,' Buttons whispered into Miley's ear.

'Let's put our gloves on first,' Miley said.

Then they started working. Some parents with children passed by and asked them what they were doing. Miley said, 'We want to give a present to nature for looking after the baby Jesus and keeping him warm.'

Miley, Robert and Lacey continued working. They were laughing and joking and having a good time. Miley said, 'I think this will be the best present ever to nature.'

None of them had noticed that a crowd was gathering. A tall man came over to them and asked what they were up to. Buttons told Miley to give the same answer as he had done to the parents, so he said again: 'We want to give a present to nature for looking after the baby Jesus and keeping him warm.'

The tall man said to Miley, 'That is something I've never thought of before, to give a present to nature, at Christmas time! I'm going back to my house now. I just live up the road there. I'll bring my trailer down and we can put all the rubbish in it. I'm going to give you three a helping hand.' The man went off and a few minutes later, he was back.

Some older teenagers were passing by and asked the tall man as he walked across the green, 'What's going on?'

'We're giving back a present to nature for Christmas by cleaning up,' the man replied.

'Could we give a helping hand?' the teenagers asked.

The man said, 'Yes, that would be great. We have lots of work to do.'

Miley's guardian angel, Buttons, whispered in his ear, 'Stop what you're doing and look around, and see what's happening.'

Miley said to his friends, 'Look, we're getting plenty of help, just as Buttons said we would.'

Miley saw the tall man talking to the teenagers. About ten other men, women and children were starting to clean up the green and the little stream, some with rakes and shovels. They waved to Miley, Robert and Lacey, saying, 'We're here to help. What a great idea!' Everyone got to work with great excitement.

The park clean-up with the helpers from
the town and their angels.

Miley's granny and grandda came over to the green too and people started to tell them the story about Miley, Robert and Lacey wanting to give a present to nature for Christmas. Miley's granny turned to his grandda and said, 'Let's go back to the house and make some sandwiches and tea for everyone.'

About a half an hour later, Miley's granny and grandda were back serving tea, sandwiches and water to everyone cleaning up the green. There was lots of chatter and laughter.

An hour later or so, Buttons told Miley to go up to the tall man and ask him his name. Miley looked around to see where he was. He saw him beside his grandmother. Miley went over and asked the man his name. He said his name was Tom.

Miley said, 'This is my granny and grandda.'

Tom said to Miley, 'You have the best granny and grandda. We were all thirsty and hungry.'

Miley's granny handed him a sandwich, and he shouted back to Robert and Lacey, 'Come and have something to eat!'

While they were eating, Tom, the tall man, said to Miley, 'I think we'll get all this cleaned up today.'

Miley's guardian angel, Buttons, whispered in his ear, 'That won't be enough, Miley.'

Miley said out loud, 'That won't be enough,' forgetting for a moment where he was.

Buttons whispered in his ear, 'Laugh, Miley. Like you didn't mean to say that.'

Tom said, 'What did you say, Miley? Did I hear you correctly? What do you mean that won't be enough?'

'I'm not sure yet,' said Miley to Tom. There was a crowd around them: teenagers, mums and dads, and younger children. Some parents had bought some treats and were sharing them with everyone. Then Robert's mum and dad came and joined as well as Lacey's mum and dad. They asked what was going on. The tall man, Tom, told them that Miley, Robert and Lacey wanted to give a present back to nature for Christmas. Robert's parents and Lacey's parents all asked if they could help too.

Tom said, 'You could help to put the bags of rubbish in the trailer with me. But there's not much left to do.'

Miley's guardian angel whispered in his ear: 'No, Miley. Tell them we're not finished yet.'

Everyone went silent when Miley said this.

'What you mean, Miley?' said someone from the crowd.

'We have to give more back to nature,' Miley said as he listened to the whispers of Buttons in his ear. 'What about some bird boxes, and maybe a picnic table or two, and a table to feed the birds, especially on Christmas morning? We could all gather here to feed the birds.'

There was a great silence, and then suddenly, Tom said, 'I'm a carpenter and I have some spare wood at home. I could make a picnic table. I have time tomorrow, and maybe during the week I could make some little bird boxes if there's any wood left over.'

Then a woman in the group said, 'I have some paint. I could paint the bird boxes.'

Another lady said, 'I'm good at making things. I could work on them during the week.'

Some of the teenagers said, 'We made a few bird boxes in school during woodwork class. We will bring them here next Saturday.'

Miley realised that next Sunday was Christmas Eve. 'We only have one more Saturday,' he said, 'because on Christmas Eve everyone will be too busy.'

'Don't worry about that,' Tom said, as he looked around at the crowd of people. 'We can do it.'

All together they said, 'Yes!'

Then, Robert's dad turned to Tom and said, 'I have some wooden planks. Maybe you'd like to come and have a look at them?'

'Yes,' said Tom, and he and Robert's dad shook hands.

Lacey's mum and dad said to Miley, 'We could help your granny and grandda by making extra sandwiches for everyone.'

Lacey looked up at her mum and said, 'What about some cookies as well, Mommy?'

Lacey's mum said, 'Yes, I will make a batch of cookies for next Saturday to keep our energy up.'

Miley said, 'I think we will be able to give nature a wonderful present for Christmas.' Then he shouted to the whole crowd, 'Let's all get back to work.'

Some of the teenage girls and boys came over to Miley and asked him, 'What do you think we can do?'

Miley said, 'Look at the stream and see if you can help the water flow a little better. That would be good.'

Miley's guardian angel, Buttons, was constantly whispering in his ear. By five o'clock, the place looked wonderful. It was really taking shape. Everyone said goodbye and went home. Miley, Robert and Lacey said goodbye to each other, and then all said together, 'See you Monday.'

CHAPTER 4

HELPING EACH OTHER

When Miley got home, his granny and grandda were in the house. He was saying hello to them when he heard footsteps coming down the stairs. As his mum walked into the kitchen, he said, 'Mum, you're home early.'

His mum had a big smile on her face as she said to Miley, 'All of the customers coming in and out of the shop today kept telling me about the goings-on down at the green. They said to me, do you know what your son has organised with his friends? So my boss let me finish at five. Your granny has been filling me in, telling me the whole story. Miley, you always amaze me. What a brilliant idea, and the whole neighbourhood is taking part. I'm going to see if I can get next Saturday off work so I can give a helping hand.' Miley's mum gave him a big hug.

Now Miley was excited, telling his granny, grandda and mum about all of the ideas that his guardian angel gave him and about the tall man, Tom. 'Mum, I know Tom was listening to his guardian angel because Buttons said we would get plenty of help, but I never expected so much. I thought it would only be some other children, but the whole neighbourhood that was a big surprise.'

Miley's mum said, 'Well, let's all thank Buttons, but why didn't you ask me or your friends' parents?'

Miley looked sheepish and said, 'You have so much to do, Mum, you're working and everything. I wanted to do this as a special project with my friends.'

When Monday came, all the teachers had heard about the gift being given back to nature for looking after the baby Jesus and keeping him warm at Christmas, so there was great chat in the school. It was talked about for the whole week. On Thursday, after lunch, Miley's teacher Mrs Greenburger told the class that the main topic, during lunch for the teachers, had been Miley and Robert and their friend, Lacey, giving a present back to nature at Christmas.

Mrs Greenburger also told the class that all the teachers would be at the green on Saturday morning to help. The whole class cheered and clapped their hands, and Miley said, 'Thank you, Mrs Greenburger, and can you thank all the other teachers too, and the principal?'

A few moments later, the class had quietened down as the children all got back to work.

The school week seemed to just fly by.

When Saturday came, Miley, Robert and Lacey were so excited to see who would turn up and what they would bring. Miley and his mum were up early. The two of them met Robert and Lacey on the green.

There was nobody else around. Miley was a little worried when it got to ten past ten and no one had showed up. 'Don't worry, Miley,' Buttons whispered to him. 'They're all on their way. Look.'

Miley looked up and saw a jeep with a trailer coming down the road towards the green. Miley's grandparents also arrived carrying two fold-up tables. Then Buttons whispered to Miley, 'Look who's coming.'

Miley turned around and with excitement shouted, 'Robert, Lacey, your parents are here.'

Robert's dad was helping Tom take a picnic table from the trailer. They were carrying it across the green, so the three of them ran to help.

Lots of people were turning up now. Everyone was excited, deciding where everything was to go. There were even two long benches. Buttons whispered in Miley's ear, and he said to Tom, 'I think the long benches would be nice down along the stream.'

'I agree,' said Tom. He called out to a group of adults as he walked towards them: 'Miley suggested down by the stream with those two benches.'

A lady called out to a group of young teenagers for them to give a hand carrying the benches down to the stream. Another group of final-year students walked across the green towards Miley carrying some of the boxes. 'The school is donating these,' one of them said, as he started to take something out of the box. There were all kinds of things, including little birdhouses and some feeders. One of the young ladies in the group said, 'My mum will be here shortly. She has special paint that is suitable and won't harm the birds. She has a couple of paintbrushes so we can paint them once they're in place.'

Buttons whispered in Miley's ear: 'Get them to find places that they think are suitable for the bird boxes.' Miley repeated what Buttons had said, and the young people picked up the boxes and headed towards the trees and bushes, and to the little bridge going over the stream.

'They look happy,' said Lacey.

The tea, sandwiches, fairy cakes and cookies provided by all the neighbours went down a treat. Everyone had great fun. There was so much chat and laughter, and when the end of the day came, everyone stood around and admired the results of their hard work. It was rewarding. The green looked fantastic, with the picnic tables, the two benches, the bird boxes and the feeders, as well as little things for insects and bees.

Miley noticed somebody was missing. It was Tom. His jeep and trailer were gone. Miley said to his mum, 'Where did Tom go?'

'I don't know, Miley. He was here a minute ago.'

Miley asked silently but Buttons didn't answer him.

At that moment, the two boys, James and Shane, who always gave Miley a hard time in school came over to Miley. Robert was standing beside Miley, but Lacey was with her mum. When he saw what was happening Robert called her and they went over to Miley to support him. But the two boys said, 'High five?' to Miley, raising their hands. Miley did the same and clapped both their hands. As their hands touched, Shane said, 'You're a genius. Let's be friends.'

'Okay,' replied Miley.

'If you have any more ideas like this, let us know,' continued Shane. 'We will always want to be part of whatever you are doing.'

Suddenly, there was a bit of a commotion and Miley turned around and saw that the jeep and trailer were back. There was a crowd of people surrounding it. Miley and his friends ran over.

Tom and others were taking out a bird feeder out of the back. It was enormous and it looked fantastic. It had a house on the top and different circular shelves along the beam. It was really heavy, too heavy to carry, so they decided to drive the jeep and trailer across the grass. Just before they did, they asked Miley, 'Where do you think it should go?'

Miley looked around. He asked Buttons, silently in his mind, 'Where do you think, Buttons?'

But Buttons didn't answer him this time.

'How about in the centre, so everyone can see the birds, bees and butterflies from wherever they are on the green?' Miley suggested.

So Tom got into the jeep and reversed the trailer across the green to where some people were standing, marking the centre. The tree trunk making up the centre beam was enormous, especially with the birdhouse on the top and all of the other sections. Everybody congratulated Tom and said, 'How did you manage to make that in a week?'

Tom turned to Miley and said, 'You inspired me so much, Miley. I worked on it every day after work. I only got a few hours of sleep but it was well worth it.'

A little girl, who looked about four years old, walked up to Miley with her little two-year-old brother and took Miley's hand. 'When are we going to feed the birds?' she asked.

'We don't have any food for them today,' Miley replied.

Robert's dad said, 'I know I don't celebrate it as you do but to me, this Christmas is very special because of you, Miley. How about we all meet here on Christmas morning with presents for nature: some birdseed, for example.'

The little girl said, 'And some fruit. Birds like fruit too.'

Everyone agreed and Miley's teacher, Mrs Greenburger, said, 'How about eleven o'clock Christmas morning? Would that be too early or too late?'

Everyone agreed it would be perfect.

'So it's agreed then,' said Miley. 'I'm looking forward to seeing you all here on Christmas morning to give nature a present for keeping the baby Jesus warm.'

Everyone slowly started to head home. Miley helped his grandparents carry their foldaway tables and his mum carried the cardboard boxes. They had to make a couple of journeys out onto the green, but on Miley's last journey, he went on his own. He stood in the middle of the green, looking around. The place was spotless. No one had left any litter. Everyone had taken everything home with them.

It all looked so beautiful to Miley. The picnic table, the benches down by the stream, all the bird boxes in different places. There were even two bird boxes on the bridge going across the stream. And then there was Tom's incredible bird stand. As Miley started to cross the green to head home, he felt the hand of Buttons around his own. He stopped and he said to his guardian angel, 'Without you, I would never have been able to do all this. And I know everyone else's guardian angels played a part too.'

'Yes, Miley,' replied Buttons. 'We all worked together.'

CHAPTER 5

IT'S CHRISTMAS!

The next day was Christmas Eve. Miley's mum had to go to work, but she finished at two in the afternoon. Miley loved Christmas, so he helped his mum prepare and he wrapped his presents: one for his mum and one each for his granny and grandda. He put them under the Christmas tree.

That evening, Miley was so tired he fell asleep on the couch. Instead of waking him, his mum covered him with a blanket and left him to sleep peacefully.

Miley woke up at six on Christmas morning on the couch, and there at the end of the couch was a pillow-case. He said out loud to Buttons, 'I wonder what Santa brought me? I didn't think of asking for anything.'

Miley untied the pillowcase to see what was inside. There were two books. Miley loved reading. Then he reached again into the pillowcase and took out a medium-sized box. Buttons said to Miley, 'This will be a surprise.' Miley looked up at Buttons, and then ripped open the box. Inside was a pair of binoculars. Miley recognised them. They were his grandfather's. Miley said to Buttons, 'Grandda must've told Santa Claus to give them to me.'

He went straight to the window and looked out with the binoculars, searching for birds, looking into the trees to see what he could spot.

Buttons whispered into his ear, 'Miley, you've been looking out that window long enough. What about your mum?'

'Yes,' said Miley, 'thanks for reminding me. I'm going to go into the kitchen now, Buttons, and make tea and toast for my mum.'

When Miley had the tea and toast ready, he went back into the front room and put his presents back into the pillowcase.

Then he took the pillowcase full of presents into the kitchen, and Buttons whispered in his ear, 'You won't be able to manage carrying everything up the stairs. Why not take your pillowcase up first and leave it at your mum's bedroom door? But do it quietly.'

'That's a great idea,' Miley said.

He went up the stairs as quietly as he could, and then came back down again to fetch the tea and toast.

Miley opened his mum's bedroom door gently, and said, 'It's time to get up. I have tea and toast for you.' When he got over to his mum, she was starting to wake up.

'What a lovely surprise,' she said.

His mum sipped her cup of tea and enjoyed her toast while Miley sat on the bed, showing her the Christmas presents Santa had brought him. He said to his mum, 'Grandda must've given his old binoculars to Santa for me. They are great. I've been looking out the window at the birds. When we go for walks in the countryside we'll be able to see more now, even the rabbits and the butterflies up close.'

Miley's mum said, 'That was very kind of your grandda to help Santa Claus out.'

'Yes, it was,' he said. 'Santa does need a helping hand because there are so many children in the world.'

Miley hopped off the bed and said, 'You've almost finished your tea and toast. Hurry up, Mum.'

Miley ran into his bedroom to get dressed, and of course to brush his teeth and wash his face and hands. Then he hurried down the stairs, telling his mum again to hurry up.

Miley's mum came downstairs a few minutes later. Miley said to her, 'Shall I call Granny and Grandda?'

'What time is it?' she said.

'Seven thirty.'

'Okay,' she said, 'that's not too early. I'm sure they're awake already.'

So Miley picked up the phone and called his grand-parents.

His grandmother said, 'We have been waiting for your call since six this morning. We will be right over.'

A few minutes later, Miley's grandparents arrived. They put their presents under the tree, and shortly after that, they were ready, so they all sat around the Christmas tree, giving out the presents. They gave one at a time.

First, it was Granny's present. She opened it and it was a new pair of gloves. She said thank you and gave kisses and hugs to everyone.

Then the next present was pulled out from under the tree. It was for Miley's mum, from Miley. She opened his present slowly. Every now and then, she looked up at Miley and gave him a smile. It was a beautiful scarf. Miley's mum gave him lots of kisses and hugs.

Miley's grandda got a pair of gardening gloves from Miley and his mum. Then only Miley's present was left under the tree.

Miley was so excited as he unwrapped his present. It was a video game. He had asked for it last year, but his mum had said no, because he was too young. But now he was old enough, and he couldn't wait to play it. His mum had also got him a new pair of trainers. Miley gave his mum lots of hugs and kisses.

In no time at all, it was five minutes to eleven. Coats and hats were put on and Miley put on his new trainers. They all headed towards the green. Miley whispered to Buttons, 'Please ask everyone's guardian angels to remind them to turn up on the green. I'm so excited and happy.'

'Don't worry,' said Buttons.

Miley was carrying a little bag of birdseed. It was his present for the birds.

When they got to the green, it was already crowded. It was as if the whole community had turned up. Miley asked Buttons, 'Did the whole town show up?'

Buttons said, 'Yes.'

Robert and Lacey were there, and so was Tom. He walked over to Miley and said, 'You must be the first to put some birdseed on the bird feeder.'

Everyone gathered around Miley as he put a little bit of the birdseed down. Everyone gave Miley a clap. Then Robert and Lacey did the same and one by one, everyone else from grandparents down to the little babies placed birdseed or a little bit of fruit in the feeders. Then everyone was silent.

After a few moments, Miley broke the silence by saying, 'I was thinking of the little baby Jesus, and the animals and the birds who kept him warm, as well as his mum and dad, and the shepherds that brought the lambs, and the three wise men who brought their gifts. And our community is giving back a gift to nature for taking care of a little baby at Christmas time.'

'Thank you Miley, Robert and Lacey for inspiring us all,' said Tom. 'Now, it's up to us all, no matter what age, to look after this beautiful green – the stream, the trees and bushes – and to take care of the nature that is around. The birds will need to be fed every day and so will many other little creatures that come.'

Everyone agreed, and with that everyone started to sing a hymn. Then Robert's family sang one of their holy songs and Lacey's family sang one too. The whole community joined in.

When they were finished singing, they all stayed to chat. Miley was surprised to see his grandmother bringing out cups of tea and coffee. Miley, Robert and Lacey said to each other, 'This is the best Christmas ever. Can we do this every year?'

'Yes,' everyone shouted when they overheard.

Tom said, 'We must make this situation happen from now on. Every year. To bring a community together.'

About an hour later, everyone said their goodbyes and started to leave.

Miley, Robert and Lacey gave each other a small present. Lacey gave both Miley and Robert a lollipop. Robert and Miley took more lollipops out of their pockets and they all started to laugh. The three friends stood on the green, telling each other about their days. Miley told them what he had got from Santa Claus for Christmas and how he was looking forward to the rest of the day, especially Christmas dinner. Robert and Lacey had nice dinners planned too. Then, they said their goodbyes and Miley walked home with his mum and grandparents.

That night, just as Miley was getting into bed, he said to Buttons, his guardian angel, 'This has been a wonderful Christmas. Thank you, Buttons, for giving me the idea of a gift to nature.'

Buttons whispered into Miley's ear, 'Of course. Sleep now and I'll be right here all the time.'

'Night, Buttons,' said Miley as his eyes closed and he fell asleep.

A C K N O W L E D G M E N T S

From Lorna and Aideen

First and foremost, dear readers, thank you for picking up this book, whether you chose it yourself or whether you're an adult who bought it as a present for a child in your life.

To all of my readers who have been relentless over the years in asking for a children's book, we hope this lives up to your expectations. Your encouragement and your interest made this book happen.

To all the children who have been waiting on this book to come out, we hope it fills you with laughter and joy knowing that your guardian angel is whispering to you, helping you all the time.

A heartfelt thank you to Mark Booth, our editor, who has been with us all these years. Thank you so much, Mark, for all the work on our first children's book. Thank you for your encouragement and for being the wonderful person you are, and for being a friend.

Billy-Bob, Jessica, Céadan and Naoise: you helped so much to inspire this book. Who else could remind us more what matters to children and how you communicate with your guardian angels? We hope, within the stories and the illustrations, you see how precious you are to us.

Thank you to our family at large – Christopher, Niall, Pearl and Shereen – for all your support and love.

We want to give special thanks to our friends – for your advice, the endless pep talks, and all of your love and support. We are truly blessed.

Thank you to our publishers, and all those involved there in putting this book together, for all your hard work. Thank you so much for bringing this book to fruition.

From Lorna

Thank you to my daughter, Aideen, who is an incredible person. You are wonderful. You have dedicated so much to this book. You have been fundamental in the editing, which I know has been very difficult because of my dyslexia, and that requires a lot of patience. As for the illustrations, your heart went into them. They are unique. Thank you for saying yes when I told you that the angels said you should do the illustrations. I know the angels inspired you, Aideen, and I know those illustrations will help children to know their guardian angel is right there with them. Aideen, this is our children's book. Your passion and perseverance meant so much to me. I could not have done it without you. Love, Mum xx.

From Aideen

Mam, you inspire me every day. I know you said doing the children's book with you was a choice, but it wasn't really. How could I ever say no. Thank you for insisting that the angels be listened to and that I be given this opportunity. I know you are my champion in this. It is so nerve-wracking, but who else would I put myself out on a limb for, other than my best friend, confidante and inspiration? Love you to the moon and back, your daughter, Aideen.

ABOUT THE AUTHOR
AND ILLUSTRATOR

Lorna Byrne is a world-renowned spiritual teacher, and the international and *Sunday Times* number one best-selling author of *Angels in My Hair* and six other books, published in more than fifty countries and thirty languages around the world. In 2019, she was named by *Watkins Mind Body Spirit Magazine* as one of the '100 Most Spiritually Influential Living People in the World'.

The people who attend Lorna's worldwide events are very diverse, including theologians and religious leaders, sportspeople, businesspeople and scientists. People from all walks of life, young and old, of all religions and of none, are drawn to Lorna to seek her spiritual insight. Many of them say she has given them back hope in their lives.

Aideen Byrne's life was transformed at the age of thirteen with the publication of her mother's first book, *Angels in My Hair* – not that life was quiet before then. Writing the introduction to this children's book is the first step in giving voice to her own experiences of this spiritual journey. Aideen now holds a master's degree in international law and is pursuing a career in law and research, helping her mother to create her books 'on the side' (she is resisting using the words 'spare time' here – what would that even look like?). Aideen has always used the arts as an outlet – illustrating a children's book didn't seem like *too* much of a stretch.

Neither Lorna nor Aideen ever dreamed as children of creating a children's book. Throughout the creation of this book, they reached back through time to thank their younger selves, to show themselves love and to remind themselves of how far they have come – something we should all be mindful to do.

Lorna at age two or three,   *Aideen at age two*
smiling while sitting in a buggy.   *or three, on a tricycle.*

To find out more about Lorna Byrne, including adding your prayers and wishes to her prayer scroll or discovering where you can meet her in person or virtually, go to www.lornabyrne.com.

Lorna has an ever-growing community on social media, including her Facebook (lornabyrneangels), Twitter (@lornabyrne), Instagram (@lornabyrneangels) and YouTube (lornabyrneangels).

Aideen shares her creative projects and insights into her life on Instagram: (@aideencbyrne) and Twitter (@byrne_aideen).